Sacred Journey

Sacred Journey

Swamini Krishnamrita Prana

Mata Amritanandamayi Center, San Ramon
California, United States

Sacred Journey
By Swamini Krishnamrita Prana

Published by:
Mata Amritanandamayi Center
P.O. Box 613
San Ramon, CA 94583
United States

In India:
www.amritapuri.org
inform@amritapuri.org

In Europe:
www.amma-europe.org

In US:
www.amma.org

I don't see into the future.
Nor do I care to see.
But one vision I see clear as life before me.
That ancient Mother has awakened once more
Sitting on Her throne rejuvenated.
More glorious than ever.
Proclaim Her to all the world
With the voice of peace and benediction.

Swami Vivekananda

Contents

The poems at the end of each chapter were
written by Swamini Krishnamrita Prana in 1984.

Introduction

❈

*"When your eyes have the power
to penetrate beyond the surface of existence,
then your life will be full of joy."*
Amma

I had always been happy being in the background around Amma, watching the Divine play unfold in front of my eyes. Not really understanding all that was going on, I was content as a spectator with whatever partial translations came my way.

I used to pray to Amma, "It is not my way to run after You, to chase after You like so many other people do. So if You want me to come closer, You are going to have to pull me closer, because I will not be able to push anyone out of the way to try to get nearer to You."

Amma used to say, "Either be one to fight and be at the front of the crowd near Amma, or be detached and be at the back; just do not be in the middle being jealous of both directions." So I often found myself happily detached at the back until Amma pulled me closer.

We all have illusions or fantasies about what we think spiritual life is like, but interestingly, the opposite is often closer to reality. The imaginary castles that we build come crashing down around us, and our illusions dissolve in thin air. Life is rarely what we expect it to be. I never thought I would find myself an author, especially of a spiritual book; but by Amma's Grace, this book has manifested.

The first time the idea of a book dawned in my mind was in 2003. I had been sitting with Amma while She was discussing some ashram matters with a few of us. Amma said, "Children, it's better that we pluck the grass and eat it, living off of that, than sacrifice our value system. It is our sacred duty to uphold the system of spiritual values. It is our duty not to make mistakes because if someone falls following after us, then other people following them may also fall."

I felt deeply inspired and stirred with enthusiasm hearing Amma's sacred words. Amma's sincerity in upholding the values of the spiritual tradition touched the very core of my being. I felt a responsibility to share these precious inspiring moments with the rest of the world. Particularly, I felt it my duty to share Amma's wisdom. For Her wisdom is not meant only for a few people, but should be passed on through all of us to lighten the darkness that encompasses our lives.

I would never proclaim myself to be the ideal spiritual seeker, far from it. But somehow, with just a small amount of effort and sincerity, Amma's grace has flooded my life. As a fellow spiritual seeker traveling on the path of this sacred journey, I offer some of my own perceptions in the hope that others will also feel inspired to lead a life of devotion and, in the same way, feel the glories of the Divine Mother unfolding in their lives.

With just one drop of love
You have set my soul afire with thirst for You.
Vainly I wander in this sorrowful world
Trying to behold You.

All has lost its meaning.
Sweet bliss hand-in-hand with sorrow
Churns my lonely life.
In my barren heart You planted a seed of love.
Now it blossoms and grows,
Waiting patiently for You to pluck it.

The lotus of my heart
Seeks its home with You.
Let not this lonely flower wither away
While waiting for You.

Chapter 1

Amma's Childhood

*"When you behold everything as God,
you are always in a worshipful mood.
When there are no feelings of otherness,
your whole life becomes an act of worship,
a form of prayer, a song of praise."*

Amma

To describe Amma in just a few words to someone who has never met Her before becomes a very daunting task. For Amma exists beyond the reach of words. Dr. Jane Goodall offered one of the best examples that I have heard when she presented Amma with the Gandhi-King Award for Non-Violence. She described Amma as, "One who is the very embodiment of goodness…God's love in a human body." Nothing could be truer than this description.

Amma was unusual from the very beginning. At birth She alarmed Her mother, Damayanti Amma, because She did not cry. Her mother was extremely worried about Her until she looked at her newborn daughter and saw Her beautiful smile. Her complexion was dark with a blue tinge, and that also concerned Her parents. They named Her Sudhamani, which means "ambrosial jewel," and this She truly was.

Amma's parents and relatives were pious people who conformed to the traditional religious practices of the family and village; but Amma's behavior was incomprehensible to them, and they thought that surely something was wrong with Her. Amma sang the names of God constantly, and Her attention was not always on the world around Her. She called on *Sri Krishna* night and day to reveal Himself to Her. She danced in bliss and made up beautiful devotional songs from a very young age; but sometimes She would fall on the ground in an ecstatic state, and this strange behavior frightened them.

Amma's village was a simple community of hard-working fishermen. It could be misleading to say that Amma was born in poverty, as we often understand it. It was more like economic simplicity with very little money, a way of life that had gone on for centuries in a climate that produced many of the basic needs of the family. Yet in village life, even small misfortunes can create desperate poverty leading to a lack of food, clothing and basic care. When Amma, as a child, saw the suffering caused by this poverty, She felt that She had to do everything She could to help those who were impoverished. This aid often meant drawing on the family's resources, such as taking food or money from Her home to give to those who had none. To Her otherwise generous parents, this was crazy behavior, intolerable to them, and it led to severe punishments for Amma. They concluded that this was the behavior of a disturbed child and felt that something was definitely wrong with Her. Yet Amma worked so hard, and the more She worked, the more work was given to Her.

When Damayanti Amma became ill, Amma was forced to leave school in the fourth grade in order to take care of Her brothers and sisters. Since She was a child with quick comprehension and a powerful memory, any further schooling She had came from helping Her siblings with their lessons.

When the children were young, Damayanti Amma used to wake them all up early for morning prayers. The others used to hope that their mother would oversleep, so they too could get some extra sleep. Only Amma was happy to jump up from Her sleep for prayers. She was the only child who was really devoted.

Amma did not take even one breath without remembering God. Day in and day out She was continuously putting forth effort to remember God by chanting His names and visualizing His precious form in Her heart. She would not take even one step without saying His name. If She forgot, She stepped backwards and then took the step again, repeating the *mantra*. When she was swimming, She would vow to say Her mantra a certain number of times before She surfaced to take Her next breath. That much dedication Amma had toward the goal of total remembrance of God.

When Amma was six or seven years old, She was already thinking about the meaning of life. For some of us, it is only towards the end of our lives, after leading a worldly existence, that we might start to ponder this question. While other children were playing with toys, little Sudhamani was contemplating why there was so much suffering in the world.

She went around to all the houses in the village and collected vegetable scraps and leftover rice gruel that were going to be discarded, and with this food She fed Her family's cows. While She was doing this, She saw all the elderly and sick people

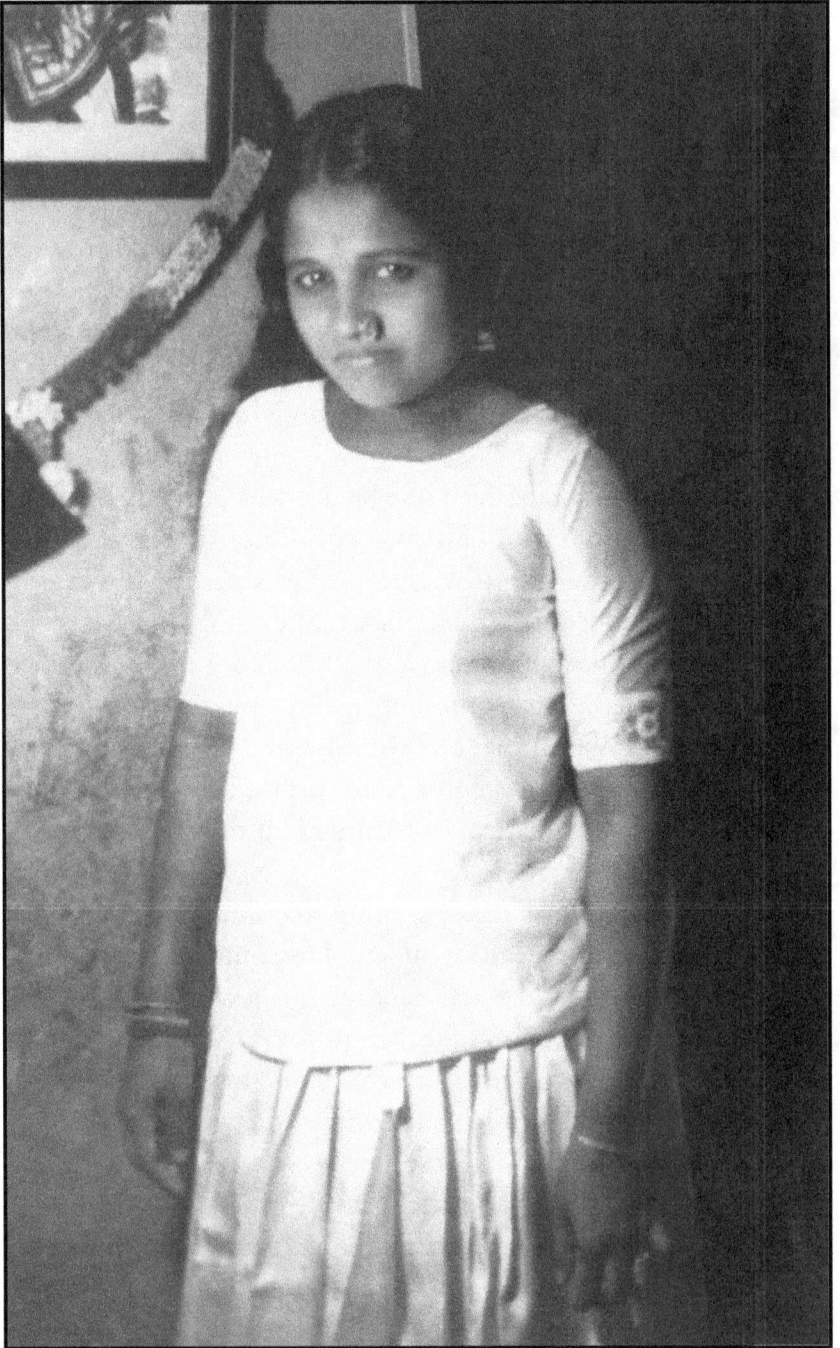

who lived in some of these houses, and She realized that their families often were not looking after them properly.

They told Her how their grown-up children had once worshipped their feet, prayed for their health and long life and vowed to look after them when they grew old. But in the busy-ness of their own lives, they later forgot their promises, left their old parents to fend for themselves and often ill-treated them. Amma, as a little girl, brought these old people back to Her own house and gave them a hot-water bath, washed their clothes in the family pond, and fed them before taking them back to their homes. Sometimes if they were very poor and did not have enough food in their homes, She took supplies from Her own house and gave them to the elderly people to take home with them. If Her parents found this out, they severely reprimanded Her and even beat Her. But no words or harsh actions could stop Her or change Her compassionate heart that ached for the suffering of others.

Because it was a poor fishing village, many people were sick and suffered due to their illnesses or poverty. Seeing all of their problems and difficulties, She contemplated and questioned the meaning of life. Amma said that She even wanted to jump into fire to end Her life because She was so overwhelmed by the suffering of people everywhere.

With Her continued questioning to God of why this intense suffering was so prevalent, a voice from within finally revealed to Her that the suffering of people was occurring because of their *karma*—because of the actions performed by people in this life or in their previous lives. The result of these previous unrighteous actions would eventually come back to them in various forms of suffering. But just as it was their karma to suffer, Amma felt it was Her duty to try to relieve their suffering. Similarly, if we are walking along and come across a ditch where someone has fallen in, we cannot just say that it is their karma to have fallen in the ditch. We must extend a helping hand to help them out, as this is our duty. From this revelation, Amma has tried to give Her utmost in every action, ever since Her childhood, to try to ease the painful suffering of life and give comfort to humanity.

People used to call Amma to their houses to sing *bhajans* because She was known to have such a sweet voice and made up Her own devotional songs. In the coastal region where She lived, each house had a book where they wrote down their bhajans.

When Amma went to a house and saw a song that She liked in their book, She would immediately start to sing it. Later when the people of the house went to open their book, they would find that a page was missing. Amma had torn out the page and taken it. Sometimes She even appropriated whole bhajan books. At home, Her family got upset and asked Her why She did this. They feared that their neighbors might come and fight with them when they discovered that a page or the whole book was missing. Amma never answered them. Only many years later did She explain that it is traditional for householders to make an offering when a *Mahatma* visits their house to offer worship. Amma could not have said anything to the people then, as to them She was just a simple village girl. Instead, She simply took a page of their bhajan book away with Her out of compassion, so the people would not incur any demerit for not offering something to Her.

When talking about their life as children, Amma's elder sister said that they often used to call Amma "crazy." Amma would lift something really heavy and say, "This is so light." Or

She would do something that was extremely difficult and say, "This is so easy." There seemed to be no reason for Her to talk like this, and it used to extremely annoy Her siblings. Only later did they realize that Amma was trying to explain that for Her, things were perceived differently. She was trying to give them some hint of Her Divine Nature, but at that time they could not understand Her.

One day the four sisters were all sitting together under a tree. Amma was singing a bhajan to Herself. She quietly remarked, "Now we can all sit together; in a time to come you will have to stand in a queue to come and meet me." They all thought, "Oh, sure! Just look at Her! Who does She think She is! She is just too crazy!"

There were many other incidents that occurred that pointed to Amma's greatness. One time Amma and Her two sisters went to visit a temple in a nearby town. They entered the temple just in time for the evening *arati*. The doors of the inner temple were almost completely closed, but the girls could see what was happening through the slight opening.

The *pujari* was performing worship to the Goddess in the temple. As he performed the arati, he was trying to throw flowers at the feet of the idol, but the flowers would not fall in the right direction. Instead, they kept landing quite a distance away in the wrong direction. He was bewildered and did not know what to do.

Amma was standing in the center behind Her elder sister with their younger sister behind Her. Suddenly the pujari stood up, took the plate of flowers, the arati lamp and a garland and came out of the inner temple. He came straight towards Amma and made an offering of the flowers at Her feet, garlanded Her and performed the arati to Her. Amma leaned back against the wall with Her eyes partially closed; then She blessed the man with a touch on the head, and She and Her sisters left the temple.

The others in the temple who witnessed this event were extremely shocked, as they had never seen anything like this happen before—a pujari offering worship to a young village girl instead of to the idol in the temple. Her sisters were totally surprised as well by this strange sequence of events, but they were also used to the unimaginable happening around their sister.

Amma performed an extraordinary amount of work from morning till night. She worked so hard, yet Her focus remained on God the whole time. One of the jobs of the children was to look after the family's cows, which meant they had to cut grass as fodder to feed them. A large group of girls would go out together, and it usually took about two hours to perform this task. From the moment they found grass the girls would start cutting, but Amma would go and sit in a corner in some secluded place and close Her eyes, sitting in meditation. The others did not realize that Amma was meditating and thought that She was merely relaxing.

The girls had large baskets that they filled with grass. They cut the grass for one and a half hours, then suddenly Amma would stand up, take a sickle and for twenty minutes She cut, cut, cut. While the others filled three baskets in two hours of work, Amma filled five baskets in twenty minutes. All the way back home the girls fought with Amma and accused Her of stealing their grass. They felt that surely She must have, as otherwise how could She have accumulated the grass so quickly? So they used to take dry twigs and keep them in the bottom of their baskets, then lay the grass on top so that they too could have five full baskets.

Amma worked hard like a servant, and She was also treated like one. Punishment was frequently heaped upon Her, though Amma never let others know what She had to endure to help them. She silently endured all. Amma used to cry out for Krishna with Her whole heart and soul. And in that yearning for Him, She would wipe out the pain of the whole day. In Amma's life the more suffering She experienced, the more She turned to God with devotion.

Oh Krishna,
I hear Your flute sweetly calling me.
I long to drop all
and rush to seek You,
but when I try to move closer
I find my feet are bound
by the heavy chains of this world
and they won't let me go.

Only my anguished mind
can try to seek You.
I have had my fill of this sorrowful world.
It still tries to serve me some more,
but I cannot touch anymore of its poison.
Let me die here alone
longing to behold You.

Chapter 2

The Path to Amma

"Life becomes full and complete
only when the heart is filled
with faith in a Supreme Power.
Until then,
the search to fill the gap will continue."

Amma

When I was a child I used to go down to my father's farm during the school holidays. There were three children in our family and we liked to help with the work of clearing the land. For us the work always seemed like fun.

I remember very vividly an experience I had when I was about seven or eight years old. I reached down to the ground and picked up a few grains of sand. Looking at just one or two grains of sand separately, I could see them shine in the sun like diamonds. I became so excited. I thought I had discovered the "secret of the universe."

I saw such a beauty in these little grains of sand and felt that if just a little particle of dirt could hold such beauty, then the whole world must be made up of such similar particles. I felt the "secret of the universe" was that everything everywhere was made up of that same beauty. We just never noticed it before because it was all mixed together. This profound insight stayed with me for some time, and it is something that I will always remember. Through the innocent eyes of a child, the wonder of the universe can unfold.

After I finished school, I worked for a plastic surgeon as his receptionist and secretary. It was an interesting job and taught me many things about the world. This plastic surgeon was a specialist in hand surgery, replacing joints of people with rheumatoid arthritis. Many people also came to him for different types of cosmetic surgery. Initially during the two years I worked for him, there were about three patients scheduled for surgery every day. Gradually the doctor started to squeeze in four, five or six patients. It seemed to me that he was trying to earn more money to pay for the luxuries in his life. Infections amongst his patients began to rise, probably because he was spending less time caring for them. Seeing this, I became disillusioned and felt that life was not about trying to make money to pay for luxuries. I did not want to "sell my soul" for money in a weekly paycheck. I sensed that there was something more to life than this and, though I did not know exactly what it was, I was going to try and find out. So I retired at eighteen.

I decided to travel, to discover what life was really all about. I traveled through Asia for eight months. While traveling I found that people seemed to have so few material belongings, but they seemed to have more peace of mind than most people who lived in western countries with all of their material comforts. This fact intrigued me, and I came to the understanding that, whatever path they chose, it was their faith in God and in religion that gave them this peace of mind.

My last destination was India. Most people I met had little by way of material riches or comforts, but they were happy. I felt that devotion to God, in whatever form He was conceived to be, united all the members of the family and infused joy into their lives.

When I was growing up, I would hear people discussing God. I did not know what to believe at that time, because no one I had ever met had really experienced what it was to know God. For me, the dryness of not having had any real relationship with God tended to turn me away from religion as a teenager. So when I came into contact with the concept of religion as taught in the Hindu tradition, life seemed to take on a purpose again. I felt that the ideals of selfless service, discipline, and developing good qualities and good habits made life more meaningful, a challenge and a joy.

After traveling to India and hearing the philosophy of life as described by Hinduism, I felt that this really was the answer to understanding what life was all about. The workings of the mind, emotions and different mental faculties were all described so scientifically and logically that it made religion very easy to understand. The concepts of devotion and of a God with whom one could develop a personal relationship really made sense to me.

I eventually returned to Australia where I reconnected with some friends with whom I had traveled. They asked me if I wanted to learn how to meditate and invited me to join their *satsang* group. Enthusiastically I accepted the invitation. As there was to be a dinner after the satsang, I prepared something to take along with me—devilled eggs. I thought it was a great idea, but it did not go down very well with the others: they did not eat eggs. Anyway, I enjoyed listening to the spiritual

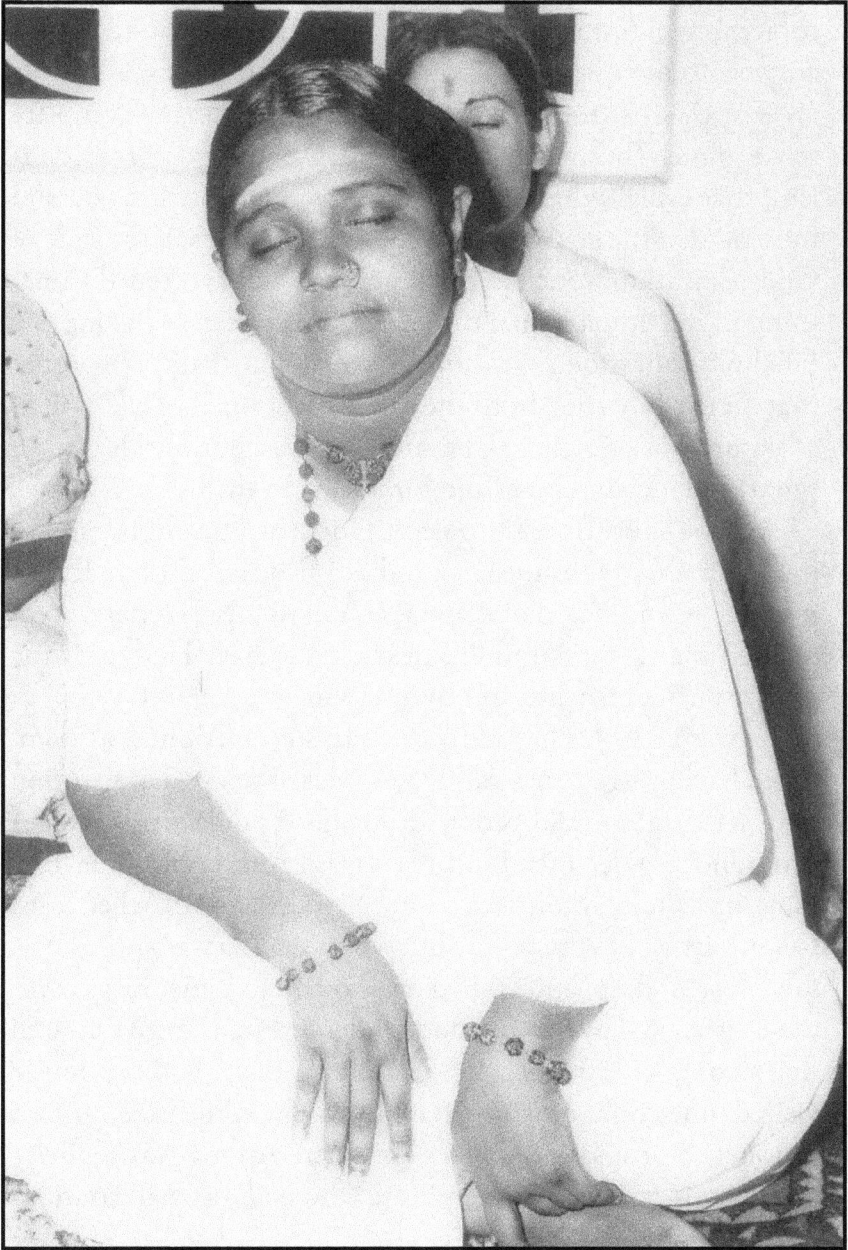

truths. That night I returned home with my plate of eggs and something else; in the Hindu teachings, I had found all the answers to my questions about life and its meaning.

For the first time in my life what I heard made complete sense to me. The ancient truths of *Sanatana Dharma* (Hinduism) that explain that God is within everyone, within you and me, and that the goal of human existence is to reach the state of God-realization, touched my inner core and awakened something in me. I finally had the answer I had been searching for. Finally I understood what life was all about. I still remember that on the way back from the satsang it seemed to me as if all of nature was rejoicing—the sunshine was glorious, leaves on the trees danced in bliss, and birds sang in the heavens above.

After a short time I traveled to India again, and began living in an *ashram* in northern India. I had stayed there for six months when I heard of Amma. I went to meet Her and soon realized that I wanted to live near Her, to have Her guide me as my spiritual teacher and to discipline me as my *Guru*.

It was in 1982 that I first came to stay at Amma's ashram. After having lived in a large and well-developed institution with several thousand people from all over the world, it was a profound and delightful surprise to visit Amma's humble little ashram where only fourteen people lived in a few thatched huts. On my arrival, I entered the hut where Amma was sitting. She saw me, stood up, and rushed over to embrace me. I was completely shocked by the love and tenderness that Amma showed me, a complete stranger. In the ashrams that I had previously visited, one could only prostrate from afar while the Guru sat untouched at a safe distance—but here Amma was tenderly caressing Her devotees, even those who had just walked in for the first time, with a love and divine compassion that I had never imagined existed.

I had read and heard quite a lot about Gurus by this time, and had always imagined them seated on a throne with people going up to them for some kind of impersonal blessing. I had even met several spiritual Masters. Although some had been impressive in their own way, they all seemed rather inaccessible. But Amma was totally different. Unlike most Gurus, She was a young and very beautiful woman, only twenty-nine years of age. As soon as I entered the room where She was, She received me with as much intimacy as if I were Her own child. "No one gives so much love to strangers!" my mind kept repeating. Little did I know then, that to Amma there are no strangers. "Here is someone very unusual, truly extraordinary," I thought.

It took me about three weeks to begin to grasp just how extraordinary Amma was. As I watched Her day after day, it gradually dawned on me that She was Divine. She was not merely a saint as I had thought at first—She was completely merged in God, immersed in God-intoxication. I witnessed Her falling into *samadhi* and lying in the sand, laughing and then crying, fully absorbed in an incredible unearthly love. As She called out to God during bhajans, Her love was so tangible. I could feel it touch my soul as She lost consciousness of Her body and soared off into some divine realm where we could not follow. Her childlike innocence would at times make Her seem like a child, the best friend and playmate of the devotees; while at other times, She would instantly become the mother, the Guru, the guide.

Amma was a God-realized soul, I concluded...and yet She did not fit into any of my concepts of how God-realized souls were supposed to be. I had read about Gurus not even allowing people to touch their feet lest they lose the energy they had gained through *sadhana*. Yet here was Amma, totally oblivious to any such possibility, hugging each and every one who came in contact with Her as if they were Her very own.

At times Amma seemed to act like a crazy girl and even referred to Herself as such. She would eat food off the ground, play with children for hours, becoming one with them, and burst into uncontrollable laughter. During bhajans and *darshan* She would suddenly stop talking in mid-sentence, Her eyes rolling upwards as She soared off into samadhi. Despite Her unusual behavior, I was convinced beyond a shadow of a doubt that She had seen God and could give me a real relationship with God. I felt that perhaps, in Amma, I had found a different level of Master than I had ever read about or imagined. It was clear that Amma had not only seen God, but that She had become one with the Divine.

Before meeting Amma, I had thought of getting married and having a family. I had also always wanted to travel and see the world. After meeting Amma, all those desires simply fell away. I had found the answer to my most fundamental question: "What is life about?" In Amma, I had found not only the goal and meaning of life, I had found a beautiful Master who would try to help me live my life according to spiritual principles. After hearing the great spiritual truths and seeing them fully embodied in Amma, I knew I could not go back and live an ordinary life in the West. I could never pretend that such a life was real. I wanted to give the rest of my life in service to Amma.

Before I found You
This ignorant soul
Was happy to wander
In the world of delusion.

But now,
With only a drop of love
From Your compassionate form,
My heart has become restless
To seek only love for You.
My mind is anguished
Only to behold You.
All else has become vain and useless.

I'm lost in this crazy world,
With my burning heart
Longing to love You.
The days drift by
And still You are so far away.
More painful is this unfulfilled love for You
Than to live in the world of delusion.

Chapter 3

🪷

The Early Days

*"If Mother's words and deeds are contemplated,
not a single scripture need be studied."*

Amma

Before the ashram was built, we had only the basic necessities. At times there was not even enough food available
for everyone, so Amma would go around to the neighboring
houses and beg for some rice to feed us. The facilities were
limited, only one toilet and one tap for us to use, but somehow
we managed with what little we had.

Accommodations were sparse. At first we started out using
one room of Amma's parents' house, but soon we had taken
over the whole house. When visitors arrived, we often had to
give our own room away, as we did not have enough accommodation for everyone. One time a family of ladies turned up
to stay in the ashram, and Amma asked my roommate and
me to give them our room. There was no other place for us to
sleep, so we slept in the small kitchen or outside in the sand.
The family decided to stay for quite a while.

Two months went by. We never complained and happily
slept wherever we could, as we felt it was a test from Amma to

see how detached we were from our circumstances. Eventually, someone mentioned to Amma that we still had no permanent place to stay. Amma was surprised to hear this, arranged for the family to stay elsewhere, and we were finally given back our room.

In those early years water did not always flow freely. Sometimes we had to dig holes in the ground to tap into the water source. Water would slowly come into the small hand-made wells, and we would collect this water to use for bathing and washing our clothes. Though the water started out fairly fresh, sooner or later it would become brackish. When we started to develop sores on our body, we knew it was time to dig a new hole.

Amma often told us where to dig these holes for our water supply. One night Amma walked past my room and said, "Dig a hole right here by tomorrow morning." I was surprised as She marked a spot right outside my front door; I could not imagine finding a well there. But sure enough, by the next morning a hole had been dug, and a pool of water had seeped through from the soil in that spot. Thus we had our water supply for the next couple of weeks. Amma knew how to provide for us, manifesting exactly what we needed.

Amma has always had Her own unique way of teaching a spiritual lesson. Sometimes, if someone had made a mistake and She really wanted to emphasize a teaching, instead of admonishing that person, She would take the punishment out on Her own body. Her body was so precious to us that these actions had much more impact than if She had reprimanded us. Once when someone had done something wrong, Amma started to beat a large heavy tin of milk powder against Her hand. When things had quietened down, I took a cold wet cloth and applied it to Amma's hand to soothe it. Amma watched me do this and smiled. After I had finished tending to Her, She whispered to me mischievously, "It was the other hand."

Amma was always trying to teach us through personal example. Many years ago, when the ashram temple was under construction, Amma was seen walking around the site in the moonlight, periodically bending down to pick something up from the ground. It was at the end of a long day of public darshan, and this was how Amma was choosing to spend Her rest time.

A *brahmachari* went to Her and said, "Amma, what are you doing? You should take rest." Amma replied "Son, Amma is picking up these rusty nails." The young brahmachari wondered why She was doing this at such a late hour when She should be sleeping. Amma said, "Many poor people come to this ashram and what if a father of a family pricked his foot and it became septic? He might have to go to the hospital and then who would look after his family? Also, we can straighten out these rusty nails and re-use them in the building of the temple, or we can sell them as scrap metal." The brahmachari was speechless while he contemplated the wisdom behind Amma's all-encompassing love and sheer physical energy. After a full day of dealing with people's personal problems and comforting them, Amma had the foresight to protect them from any harm that might come to them during their visit to the ashram.

Once when Amma was eating lunch with the ashram residents, She knocked over Her glass of *buttermilk* and the contents spilled onto the cement floor. I rushed to get a cloth, but Amma stopped me and proceeded to drink the buttermilk directly off the floor. Two visiting westerners who were present on that occasion looked at each other, shocked. Soon afterwards, they left the ashram—apparently they were not ready for such an advanced lesson.

In the old days, in addition to daily darshan and bhajan programs, Amma used to give the *Bhava* darshans three times a week. Although Amma stopped giving *Krishna Bhava* darshan in 1985, She still occasionally gives *Devi Bhava* darshan. About these special Bhava darshans, Amma once said: "All the deities of the Hindu pantheon, which represent the numberless aspects of the one Supreme Being, exist within us. One possessing Divine Power can manifest any of them by mere will for the good of the world. Krishna Bhava is the manifestation of the Pure Being aspect, and Devi Bhava is the manifestation of the Eternal Feminine, the Creatrix, the active principle of the Impersonal Absolute. Why should a lawyer wear a black coat or a policeman a uniform and a cap? All these are merely external aids meant to create a certain feeling or impression. In a similar manner, Amma dresses as Devi in order to give strength to the devotional attitude of the people coming for darshan. Amma's intention is to help people reach the Truth. The *Atman* or Self that is in Me is also in you. If you can realize the Indivisible Principle that is ever shining in you, you will become That."

These Bhava darshan programs would start in the late afternoon with bhajans, followed by the Krishna Bhava. Amma would assume the mood and dress of Lord Krishna and then receive all the devotees individually, giving them the blessings and *prasad* of Krishna until around midnight. Then as Devi, Amma embraced all the devotees again, with this portion of the program continuing until around daybreak.

After maybe an hour or two of rest, and sometimes none at all, we would depart for different places in Kerala to perform bhajans and *pujas* at houses. Often staying the night, we would return to the ashram the next day just in time for another Bhava darshan to begin.

After a short time of living in the ashram, Amma asked me to take over the position of attending to Her needs during the Bhava darshans. This was a great honor and a pleasure for me, but also very difficult as I did not understand *Malayalam*. I frequently had to guess what it was that Amma was requesting. Amma often joked that if She asked for one thing, I would give Her something totally opposite.

In those days, Amma would never take anything for Herself during the Bhavas. She would only give to others. She would not even lift Her hand to wipe Her face or take a drink, in this way teaching us the completely selfless nature of the Divine Mother. Even to this day, while eating or drinking, Amma will never consume the full amount of anything offered to Her. She will always leave something, as if to show that we too, should never take everything for ourselves, but should always offer something back for the rest of the creation.

During Krishna Bhava, a local devotee upheld the tradition of bringing Amma a pot of milk to drink, as Krishna loved milk products. Amma would not drink it Herself but would let the devotee pour a little into Her mouth. Then at the end, She would give those devotees remaining in the *kalari* some of the milk as prasad, pouring it into their mouths one by one.

On one particular night during the middle of the evening, I had offered Amma a drink of juice. While holding it for Her to drink, I accidentally bumped the edge of the glass against Her teeth. I felt terrible about this, knowing that it happened due to my carelessness. Hours later at the very end of darshan, the devotee offered Amma, as Krishna, some milk, and then Amma proceeded to offer the milk to everyone else. When She came to me, with a cheeky smile, instead of pouring the milk into my mouth, She bumped the container against my teeth. It gave me a big surprise but reminded me of my earlier careless-ness and impressed upon me the point of having concentration and carefulness while performing any actions around Amma. For a spiritual seeker, utmost *shraddha* and concentration are absolutely essential. Amma, in Her own inimitable way, was reminding me of this very important principle.

During the Devi Bhava darshan, it was my duty to wipe Amma's face. Although Her body never perspired, Her face sometimes would, as the kalari had no windows and was always very hot and crowded. In fact, the heat was so intense at times that we would have to pour water on the walls to try to lower the temperature.

Amma liked to have Her face wiped after every few people had received an embrace, and I had to figure out the correct moment. I often dreaded sticking a towel into the face of the Divine Mother, but it was my duty.

In those days, Amma often appeared to me in my dreams at night in the form of Devi, glaring at me as if to say, "Aren't you going to wipe my face for me?" These dreams were so real that I would fully believe Amma was there in the room with me. Still asleep, I would sometimes jump up from my mat and start search-ing for Her face towel, feeling very guilty because I had been lying down sleeping. When I would finally wake up and realize that it was only a dream, I would apologize to Amma for sleeping and would eventually lie down again, as what else could I do?

Sometimes another girl would be sharing the room with me and would inquire what I was doing getting up in the middle of the night. These dreams used to happen at least once a week, sometimes even several times a week, and went on for a few years before finally stopping. I felt that Amma was trying to remind me, again and again, that I slept too much.

One night, Amma offered that I could sleep in Her room with Her. Sometimes She would let us few girls residing in the ashram stay in the room with Her as a special opportunity to be close to Her. On this night it was particularly special as it was Krishna's birthday. Mahatmas never really sleep, for they always have full awareness. Nonetheless, on this occasion, Amma eventually lay down to rest on the balcony of Her room, and I lay down to sleep near Her feet.

Soon after drifting off to sleep, I had an amazing dream of having discovered a book that had all the mysteries of the universe in it. After some time, I found myself calling out loudly to Devi, with my hands together on top of my head in a prayer position. My calls for Devi had woken up Amma. She reached over and put Her hand on the top of my head and was saying, "*Mol* (daughter), *mol*," to try to quieten me. I was embarrassed that I had disturbed Amma's rest, but She did not say anything more. We both lay down again, and once again I was deep into another dream about the Goddess of the Universe.

When I awoke the next morning, I left quietly, not wanting to disturb Amma any more than I already had. Later on in the day when Amma came down from Her room, I went over to Her and asked, "Amma, did something happen last night?" She said, "All this time I thought you were a Krishna devotee, but there you were calling out for Devi!" I asked Amma what had really happened. Had it been a dream or was it actually a spiritual experience? Amma replied, "It was part dream and part experience. It is the beginning of real devotion. Just the breath of a Mahatma is enough to make people have spiritual experiences." So it was actually nothing to do with me, for it was Amma's breath that had made me have this experience.

The early days with Amma were incredibly blissful. She would spend large portions of Her days and nights immersed in samadhi. As we gazed on Her, peace and bliss would rain down upon us. When She was not lost in loving God, Amma would spend Her time loving those of us who were fortunate enough to be with Her. She could not hide this love or keep it to Herself, as love was vibrating in Her every cell and flowing from every pore of Her body.

Oh Lord of Compassion,
how did you get this name
when You ceaselessly
taunt my aching heart?
I know not of Your compassion.
I wait with this burning love
desirous of Your mercy.

How many rivers of tears must I cry?
How many fires
must my anguished heart burn?
Is this how You taunted the poor gopis
and Radha who loved You so long ago?
Have You no shame?

Take pity on us poor souls
deliver us from the world of sorrow.

Chapter 4

✿

The Guru's Compassion

*"Each and every drop of Amma's blood,
each and every particle of Her energy,
is for Her children.
The purpose of this body
and of Amma's whole life
is to serve Her children."*

Amma

The love that a Guru has for a disciple is truly the greatest love in this world. No other love can be compared to this kind of selfless divine love.

The mother who gave birth to us will look after us for only a few years; and these days, many mothers will not even do that. But the love that Amma has for us is very different; it is incredibly profound and all encompassing. For our sake, She is willing to undergo any sacrifice.

Amma is a fully God-realized Master who has no karma Herself and no obligation whatsoever to return to the earth. If She wished, after leaving Her body, She could remain forever merged in the state of Supreme bliss and peace and never return to this world of suffering and ignorance. But for our sake, She says She will return in order to set us free. She says that She is ready to come back lifetime after lifetime to take us to the goal of God-realization. There can be no greater love than this anywhere in the universe. We should feel extremely blessed that Amma has this kind of love for us and very fortunate that we have come to Her and begun to experience that love.

There was once a disciple who was living in his Guru's ashram. His mind was still inclined towards worldly desires, so the Guru sent him off to get married to satisfy the cravings of his mind, telling him to return after ten years. After ten years had passed, the disciple had several children and had become wealthy. His Guru visited him and reminded him that it was now time to return to spiritual life, but the man said that his children were still young and needed him. He wanted a few more years to raise them, and then he would return to the ashram.

Another ten years went by, and the Guru again came to visit. This time the disciple said that although his wife had died and his children had grown up, they still did not know how to handle their responsibilities properly and might squander all his wealth, so he needed a few more years so they could reach full adulthood.

Seven more years went by. This time when the Guru returned to the disciple's house, a big dog was guarding the gate. The Guru recognized him—it was the disciple. He had died a few years earlier and had been reborn as a watchdog because of his attachment to his wealth and children. The Guru knelt down and called the dog over to him. The dog said, "Master, in a few more years I will return to you. My children are at the peak of their good fortunes and have some jealous enemies whom I must protect them from before I can leave."

Ten years later, the Guru again returned. The dog had died, and the Guru saw that due to the disciple's attachments, he had now taken birth as a venomous snake that was living under the safe in the house. The Guru decided it was time to deliver his disciple from delusion. He told the disciple's grandson that a poisonous snake was inside the house and instructed him not to kill it, but only to give it a good beating and then bring it to him. His instructions were carried out.

The Guru lifted the bruised snake, fondly caressed it, and then gently wrapped it around his neck. As he walked back to his ashram, he lovingly spoke to the snake, "Beloved disciple, no one has ever been able to satisfy their cravings by giving in to them. The mind can never be satisfied. Discrimination is your only refuge. Wake up! At least in your next birth you can attain the Supreme." In that moment the snake remembered his previous identity and was amazed. "*Gurudev*, how gracious you are! Even though I proved so ungrateful, you have followed me and looked after me in every moment. Oh Gurudev, I surrender at your lotus feet!"

Like the Guru in the story, Amma is ready to wait lifetimes for us, searching for us in all our future incarnations in order to lead us to liberation. That is pure love, love that will never wane, love that bears all and is willing to wait for us forever. Amma embodies that love.

Only Amma knows what Divine Love truly is. We will never really be able to understand the love She has for us. It is beyond our comprehension, beyond anything we can imagine. We do not even have the depth to experience more than a taste of it, but even just a taste proves that Amma's love is the purest there could ever be.

At the end of a Devi Bhava darshan in India, the family of one of the girls who lives in the ashram had the chance to perform the *pada puja*. Amma knew that this family was very poor and wondered how they had all been able to afford the long train trip to the ashram. After Her feet had been lovingly bathed in curd, ghee, honey, and rose water, Amma was surprised to see the father produce a beautiful pair of gold anklets and reverently place them around Her ankles. She asked him where he had acquired the money to purchase them, but he did not answer. One of his friends later confided to Amma that he had borrowed the money, both for the trip and the anklets, from a moneylender at a very high rate of interest, just to be able to fulfill his family's desire of worshipping Amma's feet.

Amma later told us that when this family performed the puja, She felt they really had total surrender. In fact, they did the worship with so much devotion and sincerity that tears came to Her eyes, and She felt Herself becoming smaller and smaller, until She felt Herself literally enter into their hearts. She said this happened because their attitude was so completely pure. Amma says that the real meaning of doing pada puja is to worship the Supreme Truth embodied in the Guru's form. By worshipping the Guru's feet we are expressing our humility and complete self-surrender.

These people were extremely happy to have the opportunity to worship Amma's feet even though they had to go into debt to do it. Amma felt so much compassion for them that afterwards She told someone to try and find a way to help them financially without them knowing about it. Although people have offered Her diamonds and precious gifts of all kinds, the greatest and most precious gift for Amma is a pure and selfless heart.

One year during a retreat in Australia, a girl came up to me with tears flowing down her cheeks. She said, "*Swamini,* I have to tell you what just happened. Amma is so incredibly wonderful, but how many of us realize it?" She explained that she had been inspired to go up to Amma during the morning program and ask, "Please, Amma, what can I do to serve Your children?" Amma was very happy to hear this question, gave the girl an apple and some sacred ash, and told her to give them to a sick woman who had come to the retreat but was too ill to attend the programs. Amma also asked the girl to tell the lady, "Remember that Amma is always with you."

The girl went to the lady's room and told her what Amma had said. She then applied some sacred ash on the woman's forehead and cut up the apple for her, trying to make her feel as comfortable as possible. The lady remained very quiet throughout. Finally, she told the girl that she would like to have some time alone. Just as the girl was about to leave the room, the lady called her back. With tears in her eyes she said, "You know, I've been sick for a very long time, and I was so tired of living like this, that this morning I was ready to commit suicide. That was when you came with this prasad from Amma. Now I know that She loves me and is thinking about me, and I feel able to try and go on with my life. I just want to say thank you."

People have looked for countless ways to escape from the pain of living in the world, yet most of those avenues turn out to be dead ends. Not knowing where to turn, people often end up in despair. But those who have been fortunate enough to discover Amma have found a genuine refuge, an ever-present shelter, and the divine compassion of a living Mahatma. Countless people who have wandered for years in a maze of illusions, not knowing where to turn with their sorrow, have found in Amma an open door to freedom. After carrying a weight of suffering all their lives, they have finally had that burden lifted from their shoulders. Amma has given them peace.

The great Masters who have reached the state of God-realization see the essence of beauty and divinity in everything and recognize everyone as an embodiment of the Divine. They have the same view of the world as an innocent child. They effortlessly see their own Self everywhere.

When Amma gives public darshan programs in India, there are always thousands of people there; sometimes there are more than 90,000 people at a single program. Yet Amma sees the divinity in every single person who comes to Her. She tirelessly gives Her divine love to all, showering equal love and attention on every person, even after twenty-two hours of continuous darshan. Even if Her own body is in pain, as it often is, She will always be thinking only of the needs and comfort of the people and never of Her own.

At the Mangalore program in 2004, Amma sat for the program and darshan at 6:30 p.m. in the evening. At 4:00 p.m. the next afternoon, Amma was still going strong. She was not just giving darshan, She was answering questions, advising people and inquiring if those waiting in the darshan line had eaten or had taken any rest. How great is Her compassion that ceaselessly flows outward to comfort and uplift humanity.

While we were in Jaipur that same year, Amma promised to go to the Governor's house to help him distribute some money to the poor. Every Monday for several hours he would see 800 to 1000 poor people and give them 1000 rupees each. In the back garden of the Governor's house we saw the people all lined up outside, patiently waiting.

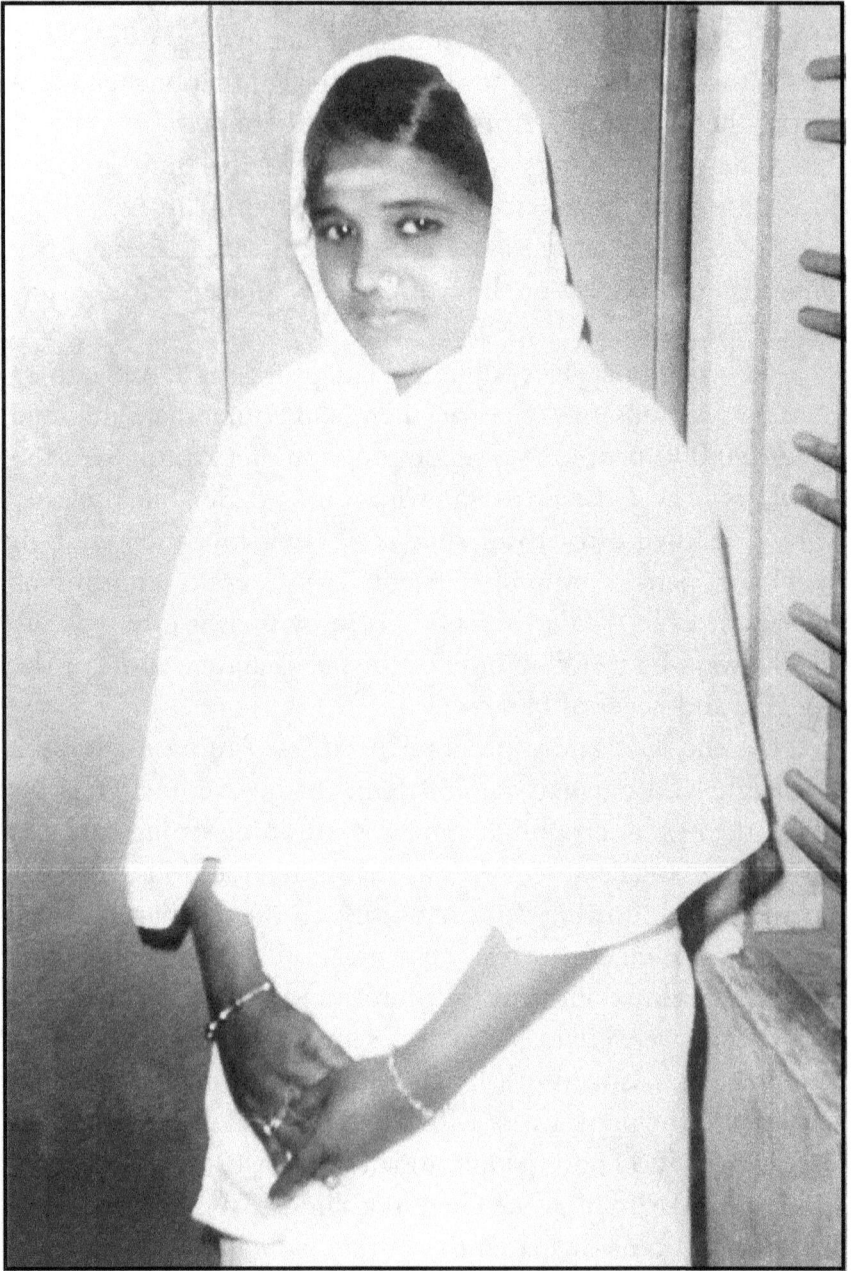

The Governor was charming, an older man dressed in a safari suit, wearing his sneakers so he could move around easily to be able to serve the people. He kept on repeating again and again, "Amma, you have shown me the way, you have shown me the way." It was so touching to see such a compassionate man. Amma asked him to give Her all the addresses of the poor people and said that She would try to help them somehow. He replied, "But Amma there are hundreds of thousands of people like this." Still Amma insisted She would try to do what She could for them. It was such a shock to see so many poor, sick or deformed people all together. Amma said that She went numb seeing them all. She can see a dead body with no problem, but to see all the living people suffering was too much.

One young woman was in a full-body cast. Her husband and family had thrown her into a well, because she had not given enough *dowry* to her husband's family. Other people were missing limbs. I could not hold back my tears when we came to two small children who had been badly burnt. One was three years old. He had only one ear and two ovals of raw flesh where his eyes should have been. It was a heartbreaking sight, something that will be etched into my memory forever. They said that the family could not pay the rent, so their hut had been burned down. Amma held the child and asked his name. He answered Her sweetly, "*Akash*," and was laughing while Amma lightly embraced his deformed body. We were all amazed that he could still laugh. He was fingering Amma's *rudraksha mala* on Her neck. It was heart wrenching to see him—all of us were fighting back our tears.

In the car we were discussing how tragic the sight was of the burnt children. Amma suddenly said that She thought that it might have been done purposefully to the children to get sympathy and money. It made our stomachs turn to think what one could be driven to do because of poverty. Amma has declared often in Her talks that poverty is our greatest enemy. After seeing this, I could really understand Amma's statement.

In February 2002, we traveled to Gujarat, where an earthquake had devastated the entire area the year before. Amma was attending the opening ceremony for the three villages that the ashram had completed for the earthquake victims, and there were a lot of journalists and national television stations interested in interviewing Amma.

No one had wanted to help these three villages, which is why the ashram had undertaken to rebuild them. We were the first organization to fully complete the buildings—1200 houses. They were the strongest possible earthquake-resistant houses as a result of the extra structural work done on them. Other organizations had come and done a little building work, but most of them had left when the costs became too high or the work too difficult. However, Amma's children stayed on, battling through all the immense obstacles they encountered. Their love and dedication gave them the strength to survive through many recurring bouts of malaria, high fever and weakness. They struggled on with the work through rain, searing heat and so many difficult situations that we cannot even imagine.

Amma's love and compassion for suffering humanity gave them the inspiration and strength to build the finest villages ever built in Gujarat. These villages are now being used as an example of the excellent work that can be done by dedicated individuals. They are used as models by the government officials to show how a project should be undertaken and finished efficiently.

After interviewing Amma, a reporter from one of the large television stations began to tell us, off camera, many sad and startling facts about the corruption and cheating that had gone on in the area after the earthquake. Very few people had received money from the government to compensate for the loss they had suffered. One lady had received 2800 rupees, but an engineer had taken 2000 rupees from her for work to be done on her house, and even then she was not assured of anything ever being done for her. It was sad to hear the plight of so many people.

The reporter was impressed with seeing what Amma's workers had done and with their unflagging dedication. He wanted to give us all the material he had uncovered in his investigation so someone could really expose the corruption and help the people. Amma reluctantly agreed to take the material, but I knew She would not use it. It is not Her way to point out the faults of others, but simply to set a good example.

That evening, the program was held in one of the newly constructed villages of 700 houses. When Amma arrived for the start of the program, the local people turned up by the thousands to welcome Her. They had decorated a simple horse-drawn carriage and wanted Her to ride in it as their guest of honor. Though She would not usually agree to do such a thing, because of their innocent and loving gesture, Amma smiled and humbly agreed to their request. She mounted their chariot and was driven along in honor by the villagers to the shouts of thousands of voices crying out "*Om Namah Sivaya*" and "*Om Amriteshwaryai Namaha*." Amma held Her palms together in salutation to all, as She was escorted to the program area.

An onlooker told me how moved he was to hear the sounds of drums beating and the joyous cries of the villagers. When

Amma's chariot rolled into view, helped along by hundreds of hands pushing it, he felt it was as if Sri Krishna had appeared in glory on the battlefield of *Kurukshetra*—so majestic was the sight of Amma like this.

There were numerous speeches of praise from top government officials who flew in especially to attend the occasion. But what was more impressive than the message of congratulations from the Prime Minister of India, was the look of pride and gratitude reflected in the thankful faces of the villagers who had received new homes. They had received not only new homes, but also the chance for a new life for themselves and their families. With love for Amma shining in their eyes, they came up to Her, offering their young babies to Her for Her blessings. They were so happy that now they too could offer their children the chance of a happy life and a new beginning.

We do not always have the chance to rebuild a new home and future for others, like some people in Amma's organizations. But we all have the chance to open up our hearts and minds to Amma's love, and to find the inspiration to do something good for the world.

Sweetness flows from Thee
like an ever-flowing river.
Your blissful grace
never runs dry.
My heart overflows with happiness
at every glance
of Your beautiful form.
And every time
You refill my thirsty cup.
To always drink of Your ambrosia
is my only desire.
You hold me in awe
and all else fades away.
What merit have I performed
to receive Thy bountiful grace?
I know of nothing,
but only to have loved You.

Chapter 5

❀

Amma's Life is Her Teaching

"Mother doesn't maintain any distinctions.
She knows all as the Self.
Mother has come for the sake of the world,
Her life is for the sake of the world."

Amma

A supreme teaching can be found in every action that Amma performs, revealing the pure love and compassion that She gives to everyone. Her life is Her message. It is a scripture, an incredible example of faith, devotion and compassion for all. Taken as a whole, Amma's life is surely one of the greatest revelations of Divine Truth ever given to humanity.

Although Amma knows some words in many languages, She does not speak any language fluently, other than Malayalam. People come from all over the world to see Amma and to spend time with Her. Some do not speak a word of English let alone Malayalam, yet their hearts are instantly touched by Amma's presence. One does not have to understand a single word Amma says, for Her embrace communicates everything. Her most fluent language is the language of the heart.

One look from Amma is enough to enter deeply into people's hearts and to entirely change their lives. Just one glance from Amma is enough. In a crowd of 20,000 people, Amma can have the *sankalpa* that everyone will feel loved by Her. When She looks around, every single person will feel, "Amma looked at me and She loves me." This is because She really does love all of us with that pure love born from non-attachment. Pure love is the essence of Amma's whole existence.

A mother's love will compel her to do anything for her children. On our last American tour, a young girl came up to me and said, "Can I ask you a question? How big is Amma's waist?"

"Oh what a difficult question," I was thinking to myself, "How am I going to answer that?" Then she explained, "No, No, I mean *wrist*, because I want to buy Her a bracelet."

Relieved that the question had been simplified, I said to her, "Well, if you get one with elastic, it will be able to fit Her hand." So she happily went off to search for one. She looked and looked and finally found a pink plastic bracelet that no one else had wanted. Just a half hour before, I had put it in the fifty-cent section, hoping that someone would buy it quickly, so I could be free from it, as it was not the most stylish piece of jewelry.

The girl came back a few minutes later with a bunch of flowers and the pink plastic bracelet wrapped like a rubber band around the bottom of the flowers and said that she was going to give them both to Amma. I was a little horrified at the thought of what condition the bracelet would be in by the time it reached Amma, so I suggested to her that she should hold the bracelet separate from the flowers. She gladly took my advice and ran off. Quietly I thought to myself how cute the little girl was but how horrible that plastic bracelet was.

At the end of the program when we were leaving in the car, I noticed that Amma was wearing the pink plastic bracelet. It actually looked very attractive on Amma's dark skin.

For days on end, Amma wore this bracelet. A lot of people were coming up to me saying, "I want to buy that pink bracelet, no matter what it costs." No one had wanted this bracelet—but suddenly it went from fifty-cents to totally priceless. This young girl's innocent love made the bracelet invaluable. Amma had graciously accepted the offering of a little girl's heart.

One year Amma was leading the Atma Puja before a large crowd in Europe. On this particular night, Amma invited the young children to sit on the stage with Her for the puja. Sometimes Amma will do this to keep the children interested, and also to keep them quiet and well behaved so everyone else can benefit from performing the puja without the noise of restless children interrupting their concentration. During the puja Amma gave each child a sweet. Amma meticulously folded the wrappers from the sweets into small paper boats and gave one to each child. Near the end of the puja, a small girl began to quietly cry because her boat had fallen apart. When the puja finished, Amma left the stage and entered the makeshift temple to prepare for Devi Bhava. The first thing She said was, "I have to make another boat for that child." She said that this child had been so focused and devoted during the program and that it was rare to see a child with such strong concentration. Love makes Amma the servant of the devotees. So everything stood still as She carefully took a couple of minutes to fold another paper boat for this young girl.

Behind every action that Amma performs we will find the foundation of love. Her limitless love knows no bounds and extends to all humanity. It is hard for us to even begin to understand the concept of pure love because our love always comes with attachments. Our love is entangled with preferences, demands and bargaining. We can love some, but not others. Only Amma can love everyone equally and unconditionally.

We witness this quality in Amma every day. I can remember in the early days when Dattan the leper would come to the ashram for darshan. At the time that he met Amma, he was not even allowed to travel on a bus because of the stench coming from his open wounds. Out of Her compassion, Amma would tenderly apply saliva from Her tongue onto his oozing wounds. It is said that the saliva of a Mahatma is a powerful medicine. While other people were disgusted with him, Mother could only show love and concern for him. It was incredible to see the look on Her face, the look of motherly love, as if he were Her most darling child.

Some may think that they know how to love. They may say, "I love you," to each other, maybe even several times a day. But if this were true love, why would it have to be spoken? When the heart is full, there is nothing to be said, for true love is beyond words—it is conveyed in all of one's actions and overflows to encompass everyone around. This is why so many people are drawn to Amma, for She is the essence of true Divine Love. We may look for love elsewhere, but nothing in life will allow us to experience the pure love that we feel in Amma's presence. Only that pure love can heal people's hearts and remove their sorrows.

At a recent public darshan, many families came to Amma with heavy hearts burdened with grief over having lost children to a fire at a nursery school in Kumbhakonam, Tamil Nadu, in June of 2004. Ninety-four children had died, and the few who had survived were badly burned. The anguished parents approached Amma clutching photos of their children who had tragically burned to death. Some of the parents had even lost two children in the fire.

One of the mothers became inconsolable in Amma's arms. She had lost her son. "Amma! Give me the fortune to see my child once again!" she cried. "Amma, I gave birth to him, I brought him up and suffered all the pain, and now he is gone. Give me the fortune to see my child once again!" Amma held her for almost ten minutes, allowing the woman to exhaust herself in Her arms. The whole time Amma was wiping away both the woman's tears and Her own.

It was found that when the children died, they were all huddled together. In their last moments of life they had held each other. Amma spontaneously holds everyone so tightly, because She knows the needs of people in fear and deep sorrow. Love naturally flows from Her.

The most important thing Amma is teaching us is how to love. It is the greatest thing that we can aspire to learn, and yet it is probably what we have understood the least. It is much easier to learn how to meditate, chant or do seva, than to truly love. But unless we have learned how to love, nothing else really matters.

Many years ago Amma was talking with me, and I wanted to talk about *tapas* and *vairagya* with Her. But She kept on bringing the subject back to love. I was a little annoyed by this because I wanted to talk about something "deeper" with Her. But I just could not get Amma away from the subject of love. Finally I said to Her, "But I don't want love!" Amma's

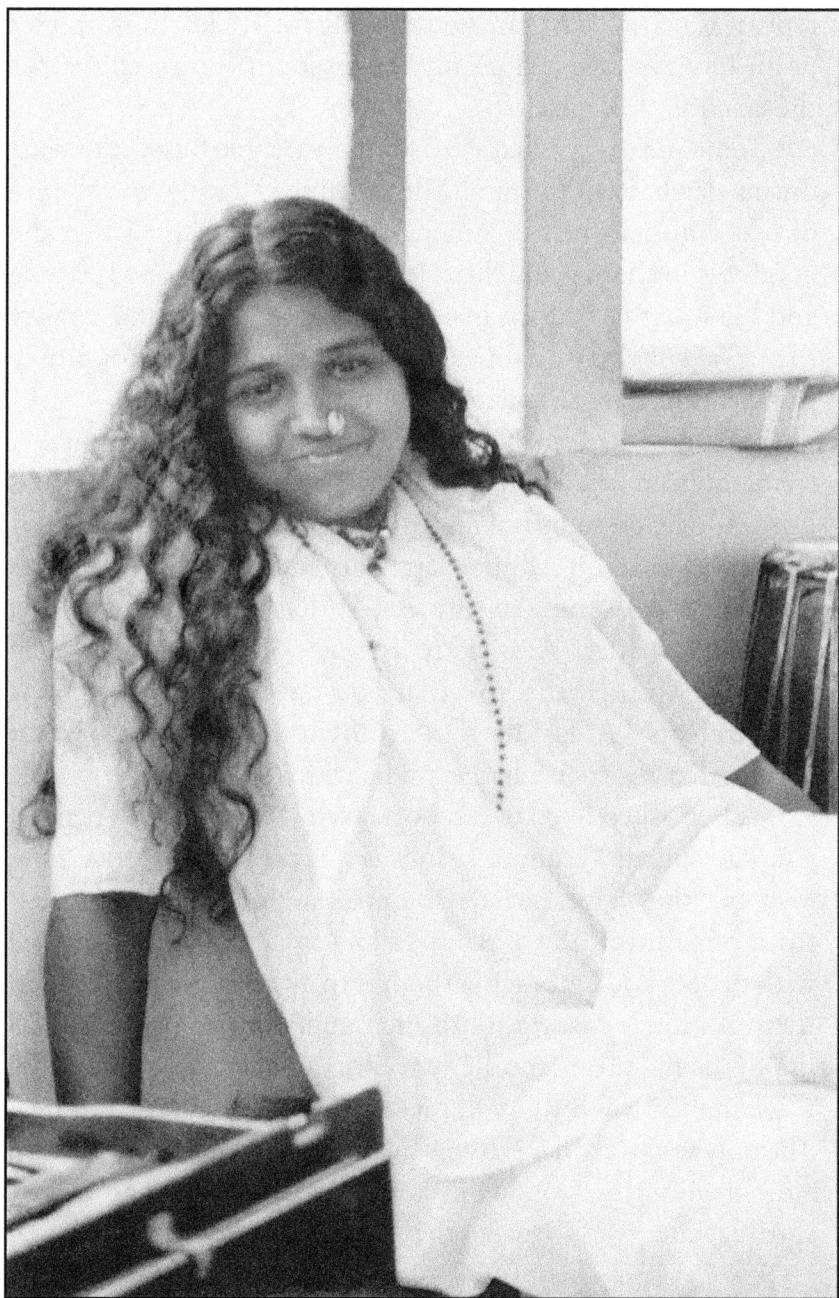

reply was, "Then what are you existing for?" Clearly, from Her point of view, love is not only the essence of spirituality; it is the essence of life itself.

Someone once asked why so many people burst into tears during darshan with Amma. She explained, "Love is the essence of every human being. When love touches them, when the goodness in them is touched, it can overflow as tears. It is love and bliss that lie hidden inside all of us. Amma is the catalyst that awakens these qualities. Amma's embraces are not purely physical; they are aimed at touching the soul."

In Calcutta, a youth in his late teens came to Amma. A friend of his had fallen madly in love with Amma and had told him about Her, so out of curiosity he came for darshan. After he put his head on Amma's lap, tears started to flow from his eyes. He asked Amma in surprise, "What is happening to me, why am I crying?" Amma's reply was, "Son, when you meet your *real* Mother, the love that you have inside will express itself in tears." At last he could really understand the love for Amma that his friend had experienced.

When asked once by a reporter why She embraces people, Amma replied: "Human beings are born to experience pure love, but they never get it. They are searching to experience it from birth until death. Amma's main purpose of interacting with people and embracing them is to awaken the pure love in them. In today's world, both men and women need mother-hood, the nurturing motherly feeling, the feminine energy. By receiving this energy, it will make them independent and free. The only way we can feel free is by feeling the love within. When Amma embraces people, She is also transmitting a part of Her spiritual energy to them, so they can awaken to this pure love."

Amma explains that no matter what problems may arise in life, faith in God will always see us through. Although this teaching is evident in virtually every moment of Her life, there is an unusually good example from Her early years. One night before the Bhava darshans were about to begin, Her brother, who was opposed to Her spiritual activities and frequently harassed the devotees coming for darshan, smashed all the oil lamps and poured the remaining oil into the sand. Those lamps were the only source of light for the nightlong program, so how could the darshan proceed? Some devotees were in tears, wondering what to do, but Amma told them to have faith and simply to go to the beach and collect some shells. When they brought them to Her, She instructed the devotees to put wicks in the shells and instead of oil, just pour a little water in them. Then She told them to light the wicks. Miraculously, those lamps burned all night.

Amma teaches us how to live in the world happily, while boldly facing the problems of life. She reminds us that although suffering exists everywhere, faith in God and Guru is the one medicine that cures all ills. It is like a life raft that can carry us across the ocean of suffering. We cannot escape problems. It may be our destiny to suffer, but Amma shows us how to face problems with strength and courage, taking them as opportunities for spiritual growth. She says if there were no problems to challenge us, then there would be no growth. Strong faith gives both peace of mind and fulfillment in our lives and provides us with the courage to weather whatever storms may lie ahead.

In early 2004, Amma visited Surat in the state of Gujarat for the first time. It is always exciting and unpredictable when Amma holds a program in a new place. We do not know how large the crowd will be or if the people will be calm or unruly.

But from traveling with Amma for many years, I have seen the crowds grow larger and the people grow more eager, even desperate, to meet Amma. In Surat this was definitely the case.

The program site was just around the corner from where we were staying. This was convenient in one aspect, but when Amma wanted to give private darshan to a few people, almost 2000 people turned up from the program site. The rush of people was uncontrollable. They ended up filling the house and blocking the stairs, refusing to move no matter what. They said they would not leave until they had seen Amma and had Her darshan.

One of the brahmacharis was holding them off at the top of the stairs, while the rest of us remained trapped either above or below. No one could go up or down. The folding-glass doors to Amma's room were shaking, and we worried that they might break due to the hysterical crowd outside the room pushing against them. Amma wanted to let the people come for darshan, but others insisted that it was too dangerous as the crowd was so volatile.

Amma was sitting on the couch and asked for a pen. She took each of the *vibhuti* packets that we had on the tray in the room and started intently writing "*Om Namah Shivaya, Om Namah Shivaya*" on each one of them. While She was writing, Mother seemed to be in another world. I felt that somehow She was channeling off some of the tension or resolving something in this way.

There was no change in the attitude of the people blocking the pathway. As we were late, Amma suddenly decided that She would just come out and go to the program. All of us were alarmed as Amma appeared in the doorway. We were afraid that She might get hurt by the crush of people, but She simply started to press Her way through the frantic crowd and down the stairs, hugging everyone along the way. While others had tried to push the people away, Amma was pulling everyone into Her arms, and She ended up literally hugging Her way out of this very difficult situation. Standing behind Her, I was amazed to see Amma, in Her usual way, accepting everything and drawing everyone into Herself, encompassing them with love, so different from normal people like us who reject and push things away.

The crowd was quite rough. One of the brahmacharis that had gone ahead got stuck in the crowd. He looked over and saw that one of the devotees had a yellow cloth similar to his *dhoti* wrapped around their legs. Looking down, he discovered that it was his *own* dhoti wrapped around this other person's legs! His dhoti had been pulled from him in the utter chaos.

We were exhausted by the time we reached the car, having battled our way through the crowd. But Amma managed to make Her way through without a struggle by embracing people instead of pushing them out of the way. Later on, someone mentioned to Amma how violent and aggressive the crowd had been and said how afraid they had been for our safety. Amma's perspective was completely different. She surprised us by saying, "Actually, it was so beautiful to see the love of these people. Most had never met Amma before, yet they were ready to wait for so long just to have a glimpse of Her. They really had so much devotion."

Swami Vivekananda once remarked, "I have experienced in my insignificant life that good motives, sincerity and infinite love conquer the world." Amma in Her own unique, very simple and humble way is becoming one of the greatest conquerors of this world. Not with a sword in Her hand, but by embracing the world with love.

I desire not for any great gifts
But just to humbly love You always.
I desire neither liberation nor immortality,
This You may give to others.
I am ready to take any number of births
To bear any number of sorrows
If You but promise
To dwell in my heart always,
And teach me to love You.

Chapter 6

❦

Attachment to the Guru

"Don't think that you are physically away from Mother.
Stop listening to your mind
and you will feel Amma right there in your heart.
Then you will know that Amma has never ever forgotten you,
that you have always existed in Her and always will."

Amma

Several times a year Amma boards an airplane and flies off to the other side of the world, leaving behind Her heartbroken children in India. Although one part of the world suffers from the agony of being parted from Her, the other side of the world rejoices at Her arrival. The actions of a God-realized soul can never be selfish; they will always only benefit the world. In that one act of leaving Her children behind, Amma gives them the chance to grow strong through their sorrowful longing for Her. Their devotion becomes deep and firmly rooted due to the heart-breaking physical absence of Amma, for Her departure forces people to find Her within.

On the western horizon, Amma appears like a breath of air to a drowning person. She comforts and soothes the sorrows of those burning up in the fire of worldly existence. To the many people that come to see Her, at last there is a glimmer of hope in their empty lives. People that have never really believed in God at last have some faith to hold on to. These countless souls are joyful to have Amma amongst them again. They have longed to be held by Her and to have Her caress away the burdens of sorrow accumulated from living in the world, away from Her for so long. Mournful hearts in India, joyful hearts in the West: all hearts are full of Her alone.

Through the years that Amma has been traveling to the West, the crowds have grown larger in every place that She visits. A life of devotion and love for God has blossomed in the hearts of so many through their contact with Amma. To see the change in people over the years has been like seeing the opening of the petals of a flower as it blossoms to greet the sun. People have opened up their hearts and their lives to take Amma deeply inside through the love and devotion they have developed for Her.

One girl who began to visit Amma during Her early tours in the United States used to turn up unkempt with wild dread-locks flying while she danced in bliss to Amma's bhajans. After being with Amma for some time, she began to dress in a white bed-sheet. She never had any money, and it was the nearest she could find to wearing a white sari—she wanted so much to become one of Amma's children. Now, some years later, she has such a strong and clear goal in her life. She has been transformed into a beautiful young lady, and she is studying medicine so that she can serve Amma by working at *AIMS* in service of the poor.

All of creation is attracted to Amma. Just as people find Her irresistible, so do the animals and insects. When we were in Trivandrum recently, I was sitting behind Amma on the stage and noticed that there was a bee crawling on Her. Another bee under Her sari wanted to get even closer. Then in the middle of bhajans, Amma suddenly turned around and handed me Her wooden drumstick that She keeps time with. For a second my heart skipped a beat as I thought She was going to ask me to lead the bhajan! But then I noticed there was a bee sitting on the end of the stick. Amma wanted a safe home found for him after he had received Her blessings, just as She would for any of Her children who seek refuge in Her lap. I carried the drumstick to the edge of the stage and watched him blissfully fly away.

On another occasion I saw a butterfly sitting on Mother's garland during a Devi Bhava and I thought, "How beautiful. All of nature wants to come for darshan." I let her stay. After she had her fill she flew away, but then two minutes later she came back for more. I started to get a little annoyed then, because everyone knows you are allowed only one darshan, and two darshans are definitely not allowed, no matter how many legs or wings you have!

Like the butterfly and bee were drawn to Amma, this attraction that we have for Her can also be seen as attachment. Though attachment is generally viewed as something that hinders our spiritual development, the bond we form with the Guru will accelerate our spiritual progress and open our hearts. Amma says that developing a bond of love, faith and surrender with our Guru is most important. This on its own can take us to the goal. All our austerities will not help us progress as much as developing a bond with a perfect Master, for finally it is the grace of the Guru alone that will destroy our *ego*.

We may perform many hours of meditation or all kinds of austerities. We can study the scriptures for years and learn to recite thousands of mantras, but all of this does not guarantee that we will reach the goal of Self-realization. When we create this bond of love with the Guru, then we can never ever leave them. This bond lasts through lifetimes and will eventually guide us to the goal.

To form a bond with Amma, it is not necessary to always be in Her physical presence. Although some may feel that it is easier for ashram residents to have a stronger connection with Her, this is not necessarily true. In the past several years, Amma has not spent more than two months at a time in the ashram in India. Every few months She leaves for a tour in India or somewhere else in the world. The residents staying behind have had to learn how to maintain a strong bond with Amma in Her physical absence. People living away from Her can lead a life as spiritually-oriented as those who live with Amma in the ashram. We can build a relationship with Amma and make spiritual progress wherever we may be.

A devotee from Mumbai told me a story about a friend of hers, a woman who had never met Amma but made the journey to the *Amritapuri* ashram to meet Her. Her friend was a bit skeptical about Amma and felt that perhaps She would show more attention to the wealthy and famous than to the poor people. The devotee was reluctant to try to influence her friend by expressing her own opinion, thinking it would be better to just let her experience Amma's darshan and see for herself Amma's equal-mindedness and love for all. So she remained silent.

When they arrived at the local train station, an elderly porter approached them. When he realized they were going to Amritapuri, he expressed great happiness. He told them that he was one of Amma's favorite devotees and that She loved him very much. In fact, he said, every time he visits Amma at the ashram, She makes him sit down right next to Her for a long time. He said that he *has* to visit Amma every single week, otherwise She will miss him very much!

Hearing this, the skeptic could not help but feel touched. Even though in the eyes of the world this porter was just a poor old man, Amma had so much love for him. By giving him such a strong bond of love with Her, Amma was leading him along the spiritual path. His simple life was made joyful by this special attention from Amma.

Amma forges this bond with each one of us, but we have to do our part. This does not necessarily mean always sitting next to Amma or performing personal service to Her. If we remember Her with love, faith and devotion, that bond will become firmly cemented. The *gopis* of *Vrindavan* for example, did not practice formal meditation or austerities. They performed all of their actions—washing clothes, cooking, taking care of babies, making butter, fetching water from the river—remembering Sri Krishna, even imagining that they did everything for Krishna. Ultimately they merged in Him because of the power of their faith and surrender.

Amma once told a beautiful story about one of the gopis and her love for Krishna. When this gopi heard the sound of Krishna's flute being played in the forest, she wanted to run to be with Krishna; but her husband caught hold of her and would not let her go. She was so distraught that she became like a fish out of water, quivering and in so much shock from not being able to be with Krishna, that she left her body right on the spot at that time. Her husband got the body that he wanted, but her soul merged with Krishna.

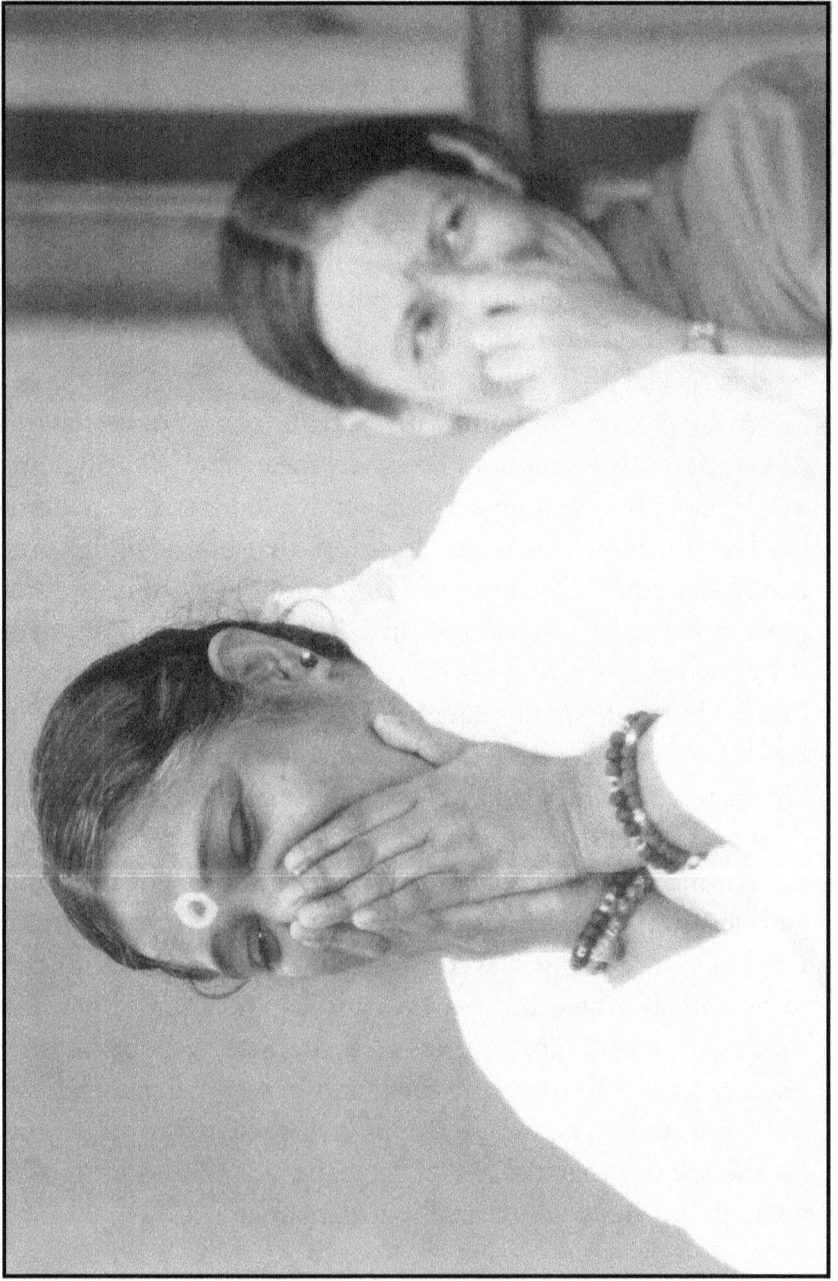

For Amma there is no difference between spiritual life and worldly life, for She sees God in everything. We too should strive towards this ultimate vision.

When I first came to the ashram many years ago, Amma said to me, "One should develop an attachment towards either Amma or the ashram." While most people chose Amma, strangely enough, I chose to form my attachment to the ashram. Traditionally it is understood that the ashram is an extension of the Guru's body. The Guru is not confined to a body, for they are the supreme cosmic principle inherent in every atom of the creation. I have found in my life that if one has sincerity towards the ashram, this will bring one closer to Amma.

The attachment that we have to Amma is not like any other attachment we might have. Attachments to name, fame or fortune will create spiritual obstacles, whereas attachment to Amma will further our spiritual growth. The attachment to the Guru's form is like a ladder that can lead us to the height of Self-realization. When we reach the roof we no longer need the ladder. Amma allows us to be attached to Her form in order to lead us higher and higher towards the goal. When we reach that goal, we are able to fully relinquish the attachment to the physical form.

Mother is always telling us that if we want to develop love for Her, we should not attach ourselves only to Her outside form; we must try to catch Her on the inside and then we will always have Her. If we have love only for Amma's outer form, that love may fade away, for our love is so fickle, based on the waves of the mind. One day we are in love, when Amma pays attention to us; and the next day we find we are not, when we think we are being ignored.

A little bit of love for Amma is not enough to keep us firmly rooted on the spiritual path. We must have strong, unshakeable faith combined with devotion. Real devotion has nothing to do with mindless adoration, emotionalism, or fanaticism. Nor is it simply following the commands of another without using discrimination. Real devotion is a blossoming of pure love from the soul—it is the grace that comes as a result of our efforts.

The strong bond that we form with the Guru can help us to overcome challenging situations and survive difficult times. This attachment deepens our faith and may help us to learn how to surrender.

In June 2000 there was a terrible fire accident at the San Ramon ashram in California during one of Amma's programs. Several people were injured in the fire. That night Amma went to visit them in the hospital. I have never seen people with so much surrender in such a horrible situation. They seemed to have complete faith and trust in Amma and in their destiny.

Amma told them that wherever they had been in the world that this would have to have happened, and that it would have been worse if it had occurred anywhere else. She said, "Our path is the path of the cross. We can have doubts, or we can have faith and surrender, and grow strong because of this. The candle melts away when exposed to heat, as also the ice melts into water. But dirt when fired by heat becomes like clay, when hardened, and it becomes strong." She told them that if they held onto the feet of the Guru with devotion and surrender that they would become much stronger because of this experience.

One of them admitted to Amma that at first he had felt some anger and doubts about Her on the way to the hospital, wondering why Amma would let this happen when they were doing seva. He also told Amma that when he reached the hospital and the doctors were scrubbing away his burnt skin, the pain was so intense. Suddenly his heart took over from his mind, and he just melted; in that instant he knew that it had to be this way, that he had to surrender. His devotion for Amma overtook the questioning in his mind and even his pain. After he fully recovered, in the following summer, he cheerfully returned to the same kitchen seva. Every year he looks forward to serving Amma in this way. His devotion and surrender in such a difficult situation became a great lesson and inspiration to us all.

Mother says that the path of devotion is definitely the easiest path. Lord Buddha once said, "It is only through devotion and devotion alone that you will realize the Absolute Truth. The Absolute Truth cannot be realized within the realm of the ordinary mind, and the path beyond the ordinary mind is only through the heart. This path of the heart *is* devotion."

In the early days, Amma told us that we should not meditate on Her form, but should choose another form for our meditation. She said we should long for something that we did not have and since we were living with Amma, we had Her there with us all the time. Mother gave the example that if we made a mistake and She were to scold us, it would be difficult to sit down and meditate on Her form afterwards, because the ego would react to being reprimanded.

I asked Amma that since westerners usually believe in God without form, how could we concentrate on God with form when we believe in the formless aspect? Amma replied, "You just pretend to have devotion and one day it really will come."

I thought of all the different forms of God and finally chose Krishna to meditate upon, but I could not find a picture of Him that I really liked anywhere. Someone else owned the only one I felt drawn towards and they would not give it to me. One day, feeling very frustrated, I prayed and cried to Krishna, "I just can't find a picture of You. I have looked everywhere, but I can't find You. So You are going to have to come to me."

That night we went for a program outside the ashram. After the bhajans had finished, we went to one of the houses nearby, as it was customary that the devotees would arrange a meal for us. When we walked into the house, I saw two identical photographs of Krishna on the wall right next to each other. Krishna's form was beautiful and I felt immediately drawn towards it. Because there were two photos I did not feel shy about asking if I could have one. The owners of the house gladly gave it to me. This became my meditation photo. Amazingly, Krishna had heard my prayers and appeared to me that very same night. Even over twenty years later, this photo still remains in my room.

I used to pretend to have devotion to Krishna. I tried to develop some love for His form. On another occasion, we went to a house in Cochin for a small program. I remember sitting, trying to meditate for some time in Amma's presence. I remained totally concentrated for a long time. A vision of Krishna suddenly became firm in my mind, and with tears flowing from my eyes I felt love for Krishna growing in my heart.

In those early years I used to meditate on the verandah of the meditation room. I remember crying and crying at the thought of Krishna while I was meditating. This was quite a surprise to me and I asked Amma, "Is this devotion or just emotionalism?" She answered, "A little bit of emotionalism, but mainly devotion. Being able to cry for God is like holding the winning lottery ticket." I had believed Mother's words about pretending to have devotion, and it really did come.

Once we develop love and devotion for God, it is something we can never lose. Although it may grow dim at times, it never really leaves us. This has been one of Amma's greatest gifts to me.

When the Master opens our innermost heart and offers us a glimpse of the essence of our true divine nature, then a wave of joyful gratitude flows towards the one who helped us to see this. When we discover our real Self, longing and respect for the one who helped us blossoms in our heart.

I have cast away the embellishments of this world
The only jewel I long to wear
Is that precious garland of devotion to Thee.
My tear drops of love for You
Form the real wealth
In this false world of delusion.
All else fades away
When I contemplate Your blue lotus form.

Lord of Compassion
How can my broken heart fail to move You?
I do not ask for anything
But the touch of Your lotus feet
And love for You
To keep me company always.

Clouds of delusion
Can no more enter my mind.
They are driven away
By Your protective form
That dwells in my mind.
All my desires
Have been melted away.

Chapter 7

❧

Sacred Journey

"In the beginning,
it is beneficial for spiritual seekers to go on a pilgrimage.
A journey with hardship will help them
to understand the nature of the world."

Amma

One night a few years back, at the end of Devi Bhava, Swami Ramakrishnananda came up to me and asked me if I still had my driver's license. I answered in the affirmative. He then asked me to go quickly and pack a few things, as Amma wanted to leave the ashram for a while and wanted me to go with Her.

It was in the early hours of the morning that we crept out of the ashram and drove away in Amma's car. I had no idea where we were going but who cared when it was a wonderful adventure with Amma. I sat in the front passenger seat while Amma lay down in the back and Swami Ramakrishnananda drove. After going a little way along the coastal road, Amma told me to take over the driving. I felt glad that I had not eaten anything that night, as I would have felt terribly sick in the stomach otherwise. It had been ten years since I had driven a car, but I was hoping that it was, as they say with riding a bicycle, something that you never forget. At any rate, I knew I had a good back-seat driver in Amma, and that even if I forgot which pedal was which, by Her grace we would surely get to our destination.

There was not much traffic on the roads at that time of night, so the driving turned out to be easy. We headed towards our destination, which by then had been decided to be Kanvashram, a secluded forest hermitage in Varkala, about two hours distant. When we arrived at the ashram the young gatekeeper would not open the gates, saying that the old swami staying inside had instructed him not to open them to anyone.

We told the boy that it was *Amma* who wanted to come inside, but he failed to understand which Amma it was. He told us that only with permission in writing from the advocate in charge of the legal matters of the ashram could he open the gates for us. Luckily the advocate lived nearby, so Swami Ramakrishnananada drove off to obtain permission, leaving Amma and me happily sitting on the rocky ground with Amma lying on my lap watching the stars.

Some early-rising local people turned up and Amma spoke to them lovingly for a while. They started to tell us about the wildcats that lived in that area, saying that they would not just pounce on you and bite you, but would pounce on you and slap you in the face with their paws. It was a little like telling children ghost stories before bedtime, but I felt safe under the protection of the Divine Mother of the Universe.

Finally Swami Ramakrishnananda returned, having received a note of permission for us to enter the ashram. When the old swami came to the gate and saw that it was *this* Amma

who had been denied entry, he nearly had a heart attack. He was extremely upset at having made Amma wait outside for so long. He said we were welcome to come in, but explained apologetically that all the rooms were locked and he did not have the keys, so there was no suitable place for us to stay. The only place available was an open-sided thatched-roof shelter. Amma said that this was enough, and when he led us to it, Amma laughed happily and repeated the *Sanskrit* mantra, *"Tyagenaike amritatvamanashuhu,"* (Only through renunciation can immortality be gained). This mantra is the motto of Amma's ashram, and conveys the essence of Her life and teachings. If She wanted, Amma could have any luxury in the world, but here She was, happy to sleep on a bare concrete floor in an open hut.

We spread out a thin cotton sheet to lie on, and I lay down next to Amma, while Swami Ramakrishnananda lay down some distance away. He had taken the role of our guard, and for protection against the wild cats had found a coconut stick broom, keeping it next to himself just in case we were attacked.

After having laid down for only five minutes, we heard a sound. Amma jumped up saying, "It's the cats! It's the cats!" Swami and I both jumped to our feet in a panic. After a moment we all looked at each other, and then laughed and laughed, as it had just been some small noise in the jungle. After lying down again for a while, this scene repeated itself. Several more times it happened. We found it uproariously funny and continued to laugh more than get any sleep.

One time though, the wild beast really did come. We heard some ominous rustling in the leaves nearby. Swami got up quickly, armed with his broom, ready to pounce on the wildcat before it could pounce on us. I too got up, tiptoeing over with my tiny pen-sized torchlight…and *there it was!* "Yes, there's the wild beast!" we remarked as an old dog staggered past us. The poor dog looked like she had given birth to hundreds of puppies in her lifetime. We continued to laugh at this, and eventually gave up trying to get any more sleep. Who needed sleep when you were with Amma?

The next morning Amma sent Swami Ramakrishnananda back to the Amritapuri ashram, as She did not want any of the brahmacharis to feel that She was showing favoritism to anyone. I was left alone with Amma. It was the secret desire cherished in the heart of every disciple to have a day alone with one's Guru.

As there was no bathroom we decided to take our morning bath in the pond on the property. The water was a little brown and murky but still cool and refreshing. Amma loved being in the water and floated happily on Her back in lotus posture. I was content to just stay at the edge of the pond and watch Amma floating peacefully on Her own, relishing the solitude of Her time in the water. When we got out of the pond we were a little dirtier than when we had gotten in, as the brown silt stuck to our skin. However we did not mind at all, because there was no program that day and no official business to attend to, so we could afford not to look our very best.

Amma was delighted to be out in nature and often looked around at the trees and sky and said how beautiful it all was. So rarely over the past few years had She gotten the chance to look at the sky without a crowd gathering around Her. Here was the Creatrix of the Universe admiring Her own creation.

We had planned to be away for two days, but by mid-morning Amma was already feeling the sorrow of all Her children left behind who were missing Her. When I sat by the

pond with Amma in the afternoon, She sang a bhajan mournfully—to the sky, to the rocks and the water, to all of creation. As She sang, tears trickled down Her face. I wondered why She cried. Was She crying for us all who are so caught up in the clutches of *maya*? Or for the ones who could not cry for God, offering Her tears on their behalf? Or was She crying for the selfishness so deeply embedded in us that She has tried to melt away unsuccessfully over the years?

Finally Amma got up and said, "Let us go back. The children are all so sad. They cannot bear the absence of Amma." I was really amazed. Amma could have stayed on and enjoyed the peace and solitude in those beautiful surroundings, a rare chance in Her life to spend some time alone. But has Amma ever been known to put Her own joy or comfort above the sadness of others?

We drove back to the ashram. While driving on the road it seemed that all kinds of obstacles manifested to test my driving skills. At one point an elephant appeared leading a parade full of people. Luckily I managed to avoid hitting anything.

When we were halfway back to the ashram a vehicle coming towards us started to sound its horn, and we saw the passenger frantically waving his arms for us to pull over. One of the residents had decided to investigate our disappearance and had hired a taxi so he could find us. Amma laughed a little like a naughty child and said, "Oh no, we've been caught!" The resident was most upset that we had left the ashram without informing anybody. He climbed into the car and we continued on our journey home.

When we arrived all the ashram residents were lined up in silence, their faces lit with devotion as they waited for a glimpse of Amma as we drove by in the car. I wondered if they realized the magnitude of Amma's love for them that had made Her sacrifice that precious opportunity for several days in solitude. Amma and I both kept straight faces as we entered, but inside my heart I was still smiling with the precious joy and memories of our laughter and the special time we had spent together.

It was only later that we found out there are actually no wildcats at all in Varkala at that time of year. And I still renew my driver's license every year, just in case!

☙

My heart offers all to You
But my mind steals back to the world.
Wake me up from this crazy dream.
I have given You my heart,
But my mind and body are left empty in this world.
Nothing holds any meaning anymore,
The world has lost its sweetness.
The only sustenance I find
Is in my yearning thoughts of You.
Ocean of Compassion,
Please shed a few drops of mercy
For this wretched soul.

☙

Chapter 8

✿

Life is Our Sadhana

"Sadhana shouldn't be done for one's own liberation,
but for the sake of becoming loving, compassionate,
and understanding enough to remove the suffering of the world.
We have to become so large-hearted
that we experience the suffering of others as our own,
and work to alleviate their suffering."

Amma

Most people think that sadhana consists only of certain spiritual practices, such as meditation, *japa*, singing bhajans or reciting mantras. However, to really attain the goal of God-realization, sadhana cannot be a separate action from the way we lead our lives. Our lives should become our sadhana, not just the few hours we spend doing certain spiritual practices every day.

Our response in any circumstance should be seen as sadhana. Amma says that we can judge our spiritual progress by considering how we react when things go wrong. Do we quickly grow angry or can we adapt and adjust to the situation? We should be practicing the right way to act in every situation at all times. Amma has total mastery of every situation: nothing can faze Her. She provides us with the perfect example that with true discrimination, one will always be able to perform the right action at the right time.

In the early days at the ashram we had no particular schedule to follow; we did the work that needed to be done and spent the remainder of the time with Amma. After a few years Amma asked us to create a timetable and to stick to it. It was a challenge for us at first, but we tried our best to follow Her instructions.

Amma always encouraged us to have consistency and concentration in our sadhana and She was very creative in how She disciplined us. Occasionally She would come around on an early morning raid and bang on our doors to wake us up if we had not attended the morning *archana*. Out of fear of Amma we would be in regular attendance for a few days, though it was hard to stay regular in our practices with Amma's intense program schedule.

While seated for meditation with us, Amma would sometimes keep a small pile of pebbles beside Her. When She saw someone falling asleep or losing concentration, She would toss a pebble at that person with perfect aim. This was an ingenious method for keeping most people awake and alert.

At one time Amma instigated a program of eight hours of meditation every day for us. However, most of us found that we were not able to do this. Mother had said to someone, "I make them sit for such a long time to help them see how we blame others for all our problems. We think that all the problems come from the outside, but really they come from the inside, from our own minds. In this way, we can see that the mind is really what creates all of the problems for us. Right from the beginning of spiritual life we can understand that all of our difficulties come from within our own minds."

When I first came to the ashram I had the desire to be able to work hard all day and to spend all night crying for God. This is what Amma used to do. I imagined myself going on long fasts, spending hours immersed in deep meditation or practicing great austerities while standing perfectly still in a yogic position on one leg. But in reality these things did not happen. Instead, I found myself working for hours on end cleaning toilets and chopping vegetables, and mostly falling asleep during my meditations.

I realized that even though we may have the desire to perform great austerities, we do not have the necessary strength to be able to do so. We may have lofty spiritual dreams and fantasies about becoming accomplished spiritual aspirants, but in this day and age most of us do not have the perseverance and self-discipline to be able to do a lot of tapas. After only five minutes of intense crying to God, we may find that our minds have wandered off to some mundane subject. The tears may have all dried up and all devotional thoughts disappeared from our minds as we start to contemplate when our next meal will be.

Because most of us cannot manage to spend very long in performing great tapas, we must have an easier goal for our sadhana. Showing some kindness to others is greater than practicing all the austerities in the world. Just trying to be nice to people, helping someone without being asked, and especially when we are asked, can make all the difference in the world. What is the use of performing spiritual practices if they are not helping us to become more compassionate to others and of better service to the world? Almost every day for years and years, Amma sang the bhajan *Shakti Rupe*. She would sing,

> *"Is it not strange if,*
> *After reverentially walking around the temple,*
> *One stands at the doorstep and kicks the beggars away?*
> *Is this not an abuse of the Path of Knowledge?*
> *What is the use of thinking of You if,*
> *While doing so, one hurts others?*
> *O Mother, what is the need of serving You*
> *If one serves others while thinking of You?*
> *Is this not equal to Karma Yoga?"*

Amma would never try to push Her teachings on anyone, but in singing the words from this deep meaningful bhajan, day after day, the teaching would start to sink in.

Someone once asked Albert Einstein what the most important thing was that he had learned from his studies of all the world religions. He said, "The greatest thing that I have learned is to show a little bit of kindness." Amma often reminds us that if we are not able to help others materially, at least we can smile, console them with kind words and try to keep their spirits high. All such actions can become spiritual practices that help to purify us.

Not everyone can go out and serve physically. People who have the ability to do so should, and those who are not able to should project positive thoughts. It is often said that thoughts are more powerful than actions. Our bodies and minds have all been given to us not just for our own use but to learn how to serve others. We should try our utmost to give of ourselves

for the benefit of humanity. Amma is always giving of Herself to everyone, providing a perfect example for us to follow.

In Amma's early years, Her days and nights were consumed with thoughts of God and with remembering God in Her every action. As a young girl Amma would finish Her schoolwork and then complete Her housework at Her family's home. But She would not stop there. She would go to many of the houses in the village and do all of their housework too.

Damayanti Amma never told Amma to do all this work; it was Amma's own idea. Her mother was happy that She was working hard, but she did not like it when things in their house would disappear. There used to be a saying in Amma's family, "Whether you are hungry or not, go and eat; because if you don't eat, Sudhamani will take the food and give it to somebody else, and you won't get anything when you are hungry!" They used to be fearful that if they let Her see anything nice that they had, She would give it away to others who needed it more.

Damayanti Amma used to keep cows and was well known for the high quality of milk that they produced. She was a very honest and ethical woman, unlike others who sold milk that was watered down in order to sell more. In fact, Damayanti Amma was so honest that before her milk was to be taken for sale, she would wash the vessel and drain out the last drop of water before putting the milk into it. She wanted to be certain there was no water at all in the milk, as her reputation meant everything to her. In the market place people knew that if the milk came from Damayanti Amma's house then it would be really pure.

Everyday one of the children was sent to deliver milk to the market for sale. On the days when it was Amma's turn, She would take the milk and go directly to a house where the people could not afford it. She would boil some milk and offer it to them. She then replaced the missing milk with the same amount of water. Amma would go on to other houses and do the same. By the time She reached the shop and gave the milk to the shopkeeper, the milk was extremely watery. For a few days the shopkeeper kept quiet, thinking that perhaps their cow was sick. Eventually he had to go to the house to see Damayanti Amma. He felt very badly about having to tell her about it, because she was so well known for her honesty, and he felt uncomfortable accusing her of adding water to the milk. Damayanti Amma would call Amma and shout at her, "What did you do with the milk?" Amma would calmly reply, "There were people with no milk, so I gave it to them."

From an early age Amma knew that spirituality was expressed through practical action. If someone was in need of something, and if She had the ability to help them, She did. Amma was not afraid of punishment. She could gain some peace of mind only if She did Her utmost to help those who were suffering.

There was once a great yogi who put his entire attention into each task that he performed, even if it was a trivial one. He gave the same amount of care to cleaning a copper pot as he did to worshipping God in the temple. This great yogi was always the best example of the secret he once told about the right way to perform one's actions. He said, "The means should be loved and cared for as if it was the end itself."

Amma says that spiritual practices are not just mere physical exercises but are disciplines that should ultimately attune our mind and intellect to the Supreme. For those who do their sadhana with the right attitude and intention, everything will come to them without asking.

In this day and age, it is often difficult to maintain concentration. Our mind becomes scattered on so many things, but it is our duty to try to control it. In all walks of life one must have strong discipline to be successful. Spiritual discipline is nothing but the gathering together of the scattered mind. If there is even the smallest desire, the mind cannot become absorbed in God. True meditation is an uninterrupted flow of thoughts towards God, but how many of us are able to stay focused entirely on God? Until we have reached that goal, we are only practicing and preparing for the true state of meditation.

Amma recommends having a balance in our spiritual practices. For example, on the North Indian tour one year, She said that satsang along with meditation is necessary even for the yogis sitting in Himalayan caves. Otherwise, they too could become deluded. In satsang we talk about holy subjects and chant mantras together. This purifies our minds and the atmosphere as well. Without satsang, we are like trees on the side of the road, inadvertently picking up dust from the continuous flow of traffic.

Some say we should not perform action because action will create new *vasanas*. But even when we meditate the mind is still active. This is simply another realm of action. So we should at least let our actions be of some use to the world by performing selfless service. Amma has said, "If you do spiritual practices without performing selfless actions, it will be like building a house without any doors, or a house that doesn't have a path to enter."

In the early years, a brahmachari started a photo studio in the ashram where he produced photos. But there was a problem—unfortunately, he had an eye disease and could not see very well. I asked Amma's permission to help make the photos because I saw how much work it was for him. I had been assisting with the photos for only one week when Amma suddenly asked me to take over this work. I was totally surprised. I told Amma that I was not interested in being in charge of the photo department and that I just wanted to help. Amma's reply was, "Who can help who?"

I spent a long time trying to understand what Mother had meant by these few words. It was like a *Vedantic* statement that I felt I could spend years of my life contemplating to try to imbibe its full meaning. After hearing Amma's words, I had no choice but to take over making the photos. We had an old, broken-down, second-hand enlarging machine and used photo-developing chemicals at room temperature. I knew nothing at all about how the work was done but simply was ready to learn the procedures. Only later on did I realize that hardly anyone ever used this kind of primitive method to print and develop color photographs; but with Amma's grace, the photos usually turned out better than most professional studios could have produced.

After ten days of busily making photos, I had not found time to meditate. I felt badly about this and mentioned it to Amma. She replied, "This work is your meditation. You don't know how lucky you are. People all over the world are crying out for Amma's form, and you have it here right in front of you all the time. This *is* your meditation."

Amma always tells us how important it is to have a goal in our lives. This is often specified in spiritual life, but unless we have a personal experience, we may not realize how vital it is. Only through a personal experience can we really understand. For me this was the case with my *sannyas*.

Many years ago I was approached about taking sannyas. I was totally shocked. I had never considered it for myself, although when asked to contemplate it, I realized that my life was going in no other than a spiritual direction. When I first came to Amma, I had wanted to have children and travel; but since meeting Amma all of those desires had simply fallen away. Even so, I did not see myself fit for sannyas. But then someone suggested, "Well, try to make yourself fit."

The concept surprised me, but made total sense, so from then on for the next six months I always had this goal in my mind: to try to make myself fit. Something was always there, churning in my stomach, and in the back of my mind there were words constantly saying, "Try to make yourself fit." It was like a tug of war. One thought would be, "How could you ever pretend to the world that you are fit for this?" But something else was saying, "Your life isn't for anything else." These thoughts made me put forth so much effort to try to do everything right.

I began to understand why it was so important to have a goal. In having this goal, everything else that took me away from it just fell away. I had something important that I wanted to try to prepare myself for in my life, and I wanted to be fit for it.

After six months, I was informed that Amma was offering me sannyas. The night before the ceremony, Amma called me to Her room and She asked me only one thing: "Is your heart open for this?" After contemplating and trying to prepare myself for such a long time, I could honestly say to Her, "Yes." I asked Amma what I could do to try to change myself, and Amma's answer was, "Read Amma's books." This is nice advice for all of us, as it is something we can easily do.

All spiritual practices are designed to give us concentration so we will be able to attain purity of mind and merge in God at the final stage. Even though we must keep up spiritual practices to try to develop discipline and sharpen our awareness, I have found for myself that the best path towards the goal is through selfless service. Most of us have *rajasic* minds and are not able to concentrate in meditation for long periods of time; but we may find that we can work hard for hours. Mother presents so many opportunities for us to attain purity of mind through performing selfless service, something that all us of can practice wherever we are in the world.

Oh my mind,
Why won't you be my friend?
We could be so happy together.
Why do you desire to plunge deep in the dark waters of maya
For such a long time
Without even desiring to break again and surface
For that pure air that is always waiting?

You know that to dwell on God makes us both more happy
Than anything else we have ever known.
What can I do to convince you?
How can I make you always share that bliss with me?
Why do you long to dwell in the mire of this world
Instead of flying in the clear pure skies?

Oh my mind,
I would give you anything you wanted
If you would only leave me a little longer
With my Beloved,
The blue lotus-eyed One
Who so often gently calls me with His flute.
Just to spend that little time longer with Him
I would give you anything.

Oh my mind,
We both have the chance to dwell in peace.
Why won't you go with me there?

Chapter 9

❦

Selfless Service

"Try to work selflessly with love.
Pour yourself into whatever you do.
Then you will feel and experience
beauty in every field of work."

Amma

When I first came to Amma, I wanted to learn how to lead a spiritual life. I had seen the impermanence of any kind of joy found in a worldly life and felt that only a spiritual life would bring true happiness.

In those early days, the few of us who were living with Amma were not quite as disciplined as we are now. We had little understanding of what it meant to live a spiritual life, and wanted only to be near Amma, to be forever at Her feet. After the first few years in the ashram, Mother started to stress the word "service" to us. We would look at each other in surprise, because we did not yet understand how important service would become in our lives. At that time, the primary vehicle for the expression of Amma's love was Her darshan. None of us had any idea that She was to become one of the greatest humanitarians ever.

As time went by and Amma stressed selfless service more and more, our desire to perform service to the world gradually grew and blossomed from the small seed that Amma had planted in our hearts and tenderly nurtured with Her love and attention. To serve the world has now become our strongest desire. In the hearts of all those who came to Amma in the beginning, our innermost prayer has become, "Amma give us the strength and purity to be able to serve the world."

One of my most memorable times with Amma was when we were traveling in the car after a long darshan program had finished. It was the early hours of the morning and we were all very tired. But as Amma is never too tired for one more darshan, She called a young teenage boy into the car to travel with Her. He sat in the car next to Her and said, "Amma, please promise me that you will take a vacation some day."

Amma laughed and pulled his head down onto Her shoulder. She then said, "Son, this *is* Amma's vacation. We come into this world with nothing and we go out of this world again with nothing. The body will get diseases, even if we take lots of rest, and it will collapse when the time comes, no matter what we may do. Let us at least try to do some good things in life, something good for the world while we are here, to try and show our gratitude."

I felt so blessed to hear these words. It was like overhearing the teachings of Lord Krishna to *Arjuna* on the battlefield. Amma was the Divine Guru imparting words of wisdom to the disciple, the loving mother advising her beloved child, and also a dear friend sharing some good advice. To think about these few sentences was to contemplate all of the greatest spiritual teachings encompassed in a nutshell. Truly, Amma is one of the greatest Mahatmas ever to have walked on this earth, disguising Her greatness in a simple white sari.

Amma reminds us that one day this body is going to wear out; we will all die sometime. Isn't it better to have the body wear out doing something good, rather than just rusting away? Even when we sit quietly trying to meditate, thoughts will still come continuously into our minds. Therefore, we should try to use our bodies and our minds in such a way that we can benefit others.

It is difficult for most of us to attain concentration of mind through other forms of sadhana. Thus, selfless service becomes our primary spiritual practice. We may not have enough focus to offer all of our thoughts to the Lord during meditation, so our work tends to become our worship and sacred offering. Amma gives us the means to attain a pure and one-pointed mind through the vehicle of selfless service, and She is constantly trying to inspire us to live our lives based on this principle.

Everything we take from life somehow creates a karmic debt for us. We should try to find joy in life by repaying that debt with love and gratitude. We should not sit idle but should work hard with whatever talents we have. We have such a great capacity of hidden talents inside of us that should be brought out and used for service. Life is a precious gift that is given to us not for the fulfillment of our own sense pleasures, but for performing good deeds in the world. We should not let our gifts and talents go to waste.

During the North India Tour one year we visited Mananthavadi, which Amma always calls *Anandavadi*, meaning "blissful place." As Amma's car rolled up the hill, the *Adivasi* people were waiting to give their traditional welcome. They danced in front of the car with joy. Old ladies were dressed in white clothes. Their clothing was old and worn, but was fluttering around them as they happily danced for Amma. She had arrived for a three-day visit to wipe away their tears and take away their burdens, and many were the burdens they carried.

Life is hard for these people who live in the tea and coffee hill stations of Kerala. Most people have no jobs. Often, the crops rot on the hillsides because there is no one to buy what they yield. Lower prices in other areas have taken away all the business. When one can buy elsewhere for cheaper, who would think to give business to the poor people just because they need it? Very few people, unfortunately. The poor farmers have no one to buy their crops, and without business they cannot employ anyone to work for them.

As we inched up the hill in Amma's car, the dancers waved their hands in the air in simple dance gestures. One short old man of about eighty years wanted to dance for Amma too. He clutched an umbrella in one hand and not quite as gracefully as the ladies, jumped up and down, the large faded-pink turban on his head adding to the comic scene as it bobbed up and down along with him. One of the organizers was trying to push him out of the way every minute, but he always managed to jump back in front of the car.

Amma said that these people had the innocence of small children. Grace is drawn from the Master by one's innocent attitude. These poor village people knew the blessings that they were receiving from a Divine Being, so their hearts, minds, and bodies all danced in joy, bathed in the sweetness of their Divine Mother's love. Amma said that many people here would press just a single hard-earned rupee into Her hand during darshan. Inspired by Amma they also wanted to give, even though they had nothing. Their one-rupee coin was undoubtedly being turned into gold, as it was all they had, more valuable than millions from one who has so much.

Everyone is always happy to visit this place where the air and surroundings are so clean and pure, and the simple sweetness on everyone's face is a joy to behold. During Amma's program the countryside is converted into Her traveling ashram. People are busy everywhere looking after the needs of others. Mantras fill the air either in the form of Sanskrit chanting or the singing of ecstatic bhajans glorifying the name of God. The vibrations purify the whole countryside, perhaps the whole country, and even possibly the whole world.

The first day of the program I looked out of the window of my room and saw that it was a beautiful day and a beautiful world outside. I could see the line of devotees volunteering at the canteen. They smilingly spooned out portions of simple, nutritious food to the hungry people lined up to be fed. Those devotees serving were happy to serve other devotees. What greater blessing is there than to feed the devotees of God? The people receiving the food were happy, because they knew that the few small coins they had given for the meal would go towards the service of suffering people through Amma's chain of charitable projects.

What an incredible cycle of service that Amma has created! It is truly an "everybody wins" situation. Those who work hard to do some service get rewarded by future good karma to come, as well as instant gratification. Those who give money to buy something get the joy from the items that they receive, in addition to the knowledge that all the funds go towards a good cause. They create good karma by providing the funds to serve. And the poor people who receive the help from Amma's charitable services have earned, through previous actions, the merit to be helped. This cycle of service brings joy to everyone.

We never know how selfless service will affect us. Only for the better undoubtedly, and in some cases it may even save our lives. There is a story about two men who were traveling together on a bitterly cold day. Snow was falling heavily and both men were nearly frozen. It was then that they saw someone lying in the snow almost dead. One of the men suggested that they save the frozen man, but his companion continued on his way, saying that it was better that they save themselves.

Neglecting his friend's advice he picked up the dying person and struggled along, holding the frozen body on his back. He labored on with this heavy burden, and after some time came upon his original companion—he had frozen to death. Yet the compassionate man had grown warm, due to his effort of carrying the stranger on his shoulder—and the stranger received that warmth and began to revive. Through his kind and selfless action, both of their lives were saved.

Seva can give new meaning to our existence. An eighty-six-year-old woman living in Chennai had become depressed and felt she had no reason to wake up in the morning, no reason even for living. She had wanted to help out with some local service organizations, but they would only accept monetary donations. Then she found out that she could stitch some small bags and purses and donate them to Amma, and then these items could be sold to raise money for Amma's charities. This woman had broken her hip, and surprisingly, at eighty-six years of age, was still using an old treadle sewing machine. Though it seemed like hard work for her, she eagerly looked forward to the idea of being able to physically contribute to helping others. This sewing work restored a sense of meaning

and purpose to her life. Every morning she joyfully looked forward to making something new. One time she sent some of the items to be given to Amma during darshan. Amma said She could feel the love that went into making the bags. She spent a lot of time happily looking at them and sent some prasad back for the lady who made them, as the old woman was unable to travel to see Amma.

People willing to do selfless work are more valuable than gold. A resident of the ashram once told me about a large service organization that had only 100 life-members to help with all of their service work. Someone had given them a large cheque, but the organization responded by saying, "We don't need the money, just give us five selfless workers. This would be so much more valuable for us." Money will come and go, it can often be easily obtained; but selfless workers are very hard to find.

"Our wealth lies in what we can do for others," said Sir Edmund Hilary, who is well known for the great achievement of being one of the first men to climb Mt. Everest and also for being one of the first to reach the North and South Poles. For most people there could be no greater goal to attain in their lives than scaling the world's highest mountain and reaching the ends of the earth. But when asked what he felt was his greatest achievement, Sir Edmund Hillary did not even mention these things. He said that for him the greatest achievement was helping the Sherpas, the native tribal people in Nepal. He further replied, "When I look back over my life, I have little doubt that the most worthwhile things I have done have not been standing on the summits of mountains or on the North and South Poles, great adventures though they were. My most important projects have been the building and maintaining of schools and medical clinics for the poor people in the Himalayas."

We may not have the strength or energy to be able to climb to the height of the world's tallest mountain, but we do have the capability to reach the height of spirituality. This lies within the grasp of every one of us. Tremendous strength lies within us; we just rarely tap into this reservoir of divine energy.

Amma consistently demonstrates the ability to access an immeasurable resource of energy and compassion. After a program of giving darshan to 20,000 people in Sivakasi, Tamil Nadu, Amma went to visit Anbu Illam, a home for the elderly managed by the ashram. It was 4:30 a.m. and all the residents were thrilled to have Her visit. Freshly bathed and wearing their best clothes, they were all up and ready to catch a glimpse of Amma.

Amma went to visit them in each of their rooms. In the first room She discovered that some of the bedding was dirty and the windows needed cleaning. In other rooms there were cobwebs and even a small beehive that had started to form on one of the tube lights. Amma started to dust and clean, working Her way through every single room of the building. She would not let any of the staff help, insisting on cleaning everything Herself. She scolded the doctor and the man in charge, saying that it was great *punyam* to be able to serve old people who could not do things for themselves. She told them that they should make special efforts to provide a clean environment for these people in the later years of their lives. Amma spent the night there, and the residents were so happy to have Her stay with them. They asked permission to be photographed with Amma, and She graciously consented, fulfilling their desire by joining them for a group photograph.

It was on Her 45th Birthday that Amma fulfilled a desire of mine. I had always longed for the chance to serve food to people. "The servant of servants" is what Amma calls Herself sometimes. To serve the "servants of the servant of servants" seemed to me a very great thing, one of the greatest blessings one could receive. As I have always been shy, I had never found the chance to do this job of serving the devotees, though I had thought about it often. It was simply a desire I had held in my heart for a long time.

I had planned ahead and made the resolve that on Amma's birthday I would go out and serve food. Under the cover of thousands of people, surely no one would notice me. Working up the courage, I went over and asked the girls in the serving line if I could serve something. They reluctantly agreed, as they had really wanted to keep the work for themselves. Figuring out that giving the *pappadams* would be the easiest, I started to do this job. The girl whose job I had taken said that she had also been looking forward to getting the chance to serve the devotees.

Was this a contagious disease spreading around? It seemed that everyone wanted the chance to serve in one way or another. There were many people, both with and without volunteer badges, working really hard for long, long hours—but they looked so happy. There is a well-known saying, "It is greater to give than to receive," and it seemed on this day that people were really experiencing this. Amma has said that just as one offers a flower to God with devotion, unintentionally one will receive the fragrance and the beauty of the flower first. In the same way, when we do an act of service selflessly, we will experience the benefit of it even before the one we are serving.

People are often shy to go for Amma's darshan if they have been working hard and do not have time to change their clothes. But Amma says that the perspiration of the devotees is like perfume for Her. It is the effort and selfless attitude that they have put into their hard work that becomes like a perfume, because it is used to give joy to others, to bring some light to the life of so many people who are suffering.

Many times we have seen Amma setting the example, coming and joining to help with the work to be done, carrying bricks and rocks on Her head or helping to move dirt and sand from one place to another. We can learn so much from watching Amma. She works with such concentration and joy. In the olden days when the temple was being built, the bell would ring, not for class, but for cement seva. When we were building the ashram, Amma said that we should do all of the work ourselves, because then we would feel satisfaction, joy and fulfillment out of helping to build. We would even feel a part of ourselves go into the building; the foundation of the temple was built with love as well as cement. We would have cement on our hands, on our clothes and in our hair from passing the cement *chatti* to each other. Sometimes it would even last for weeks afterwards to remind us of these times. But there is always great happiness when we are able to work hard for a good cause.

Amma does not have to see us working for us to receive Her grace. It is an automatic cosmic law that if you are working selflessly to serve the Guru at any time or place, even if unseen, then the Guru's grace will flow towards you. Mother says that Her blessings have to flow to those who are doing selfless work and putting forth effort, no matter what type of people they are.

As the years have gone by, it has been so wonderful to see a change in people. Upon their first meeting with Amma, many devotees want only to sit near Amma and gaze at Her.

After some time, they discover the bliss of selfless service and become ready to spend more of their time away from Amma, doing the work that needs to be done. They are happy to do the smaller jobs that no one else wants to do, just as much as the seemingly more important jobs around Amma. Whatever job we are given to do, we have to try and utilize it as a means to become humble, to develop our shraddha, and to offer service to the world. If you have love in your heart for Amma and offer your work to Her, then you will certainly receive Her grace.

The Amritapuri ashram has grown entirely out of love for Amma. She has entrusted many of us with responsibilities far beyond our capabilities; but through Her grace we have been molded and trained until we could do the job. For example, it was a baker's son who helped to build the AIMS hospital on land that was formerly a swamp. He had no prior experience in building, but Amma guided him along the way to help create a medical empire.

When the ashram first started its own press, the boy appointed to be in charge knew nothing about how to run it. Now the press is actively and successfully publishing books that are distributed in different languages within India and all over the world.

Amma reminds us that we should work hard without thinking of the result of our effort. What is needed is our sincerity. Once we have the proper attitude and the willingness, Amma's grace becomes the vehicle that enables us to serve.

I search the empty skies – but I never see You.
I turn around with my breath held in anticipation,
but You are never behind me.
My teardrops are my constant companions –
we wait together hoping one day to find You.
I ask the blades of grass if You have ever walked by
but they have never seen You.
Of what use is my voice
if my cries for You can never be heard?

Of what use are my eyes
if they will never behold You?
Of what use are my hands
if they can never touch Your holy feet?
Where do You dwell my Beloved
who has so cruelly forsaken me?

Chapter 10

⚘

Effort and Grace

"Self-effort and grace are interdependent.
Without one, the other is impossible."

Amma

The grace of the Guru is one of life's most wonderful gifts. Spiritual seekers strive hard to attain it, but it is not always so easily attained. One cannot say exactly how grace will manifest, but Amma has given us many hints on how to become deserving of it. First we have to put in the effort, and only then will grace come. It is not that grace flows only at certain times and not at others. Amma assures us that Her grace is always present, but to feel it we have to do our part. Our hard work acts as the essential catalyst that allows for grace to flow.

We are all just beginners in spiritual life. Even after many years of performing spiritual practices, we still find that the goal is very far away. It is impossible to become Self-realized by our own endeavors, but with the Guru's grace we can become liberated. It is my belief that if we try to lead a good life, then with the grace of the Guru we will reach the goal at the end of our life. Still, we must put forth immense effort. We cannot sit by idly waiting for that final moment of grace to come, but we should work hard to be worthy of that flood of grace to come to us in the end.

To attain that goal, we have to burn up every negative tendency within us—anger, greed, lust, pride, etc. How difficult it is to get rid of even one! Yet we should endeavor to work hard to get rid of our vasanas and really try to become pure. Then, just as Amma offers Herself to the world, we too will be able to offer something precious back.

Amma says that we will not be able to make any spiritual progress without persistence. Only when we honestly strive hard for the goal will grace flow to us. Sometimes we are ready to put forth a little effort, and we find we receive just a little grace. But for grace to fill our lives, we will have to persevere relentlessly.

In this day and age there is so much new technological machinery and equipment to run tests for diagnosing illnesses. For the tests to work effectively, the patients have to do something to prepare for them, such as drinking large amounts of water or fasting. Similarly, the Guru can do a lot for us, but we still have to do our part as well.

We were once in an airport and wanted to take Amma to a lounge upstairs. Amma and Her attendant got onto the elevator, but Her attendant forgot to press the button for the second floor. They were standing there in the elevator for a long time, going neither up nor down, before they realized what had happened. It was a great example for showing how we cannot rise in spiritual life unless we strive with persistence.

Our continuous attempts, even if small, will someday bear fruit. Take the example of a tiny plant growing in a small crack in the sidewalk. Although the cement seems infinitely stronger than the seedling, one day that cement slab may completely break apart just because of the steady growth of that little plant. Likewise, the cement of our ego will also crack one day. All we need to do is work hard with patience and discipline.

There is a story about Beethoven that illustrates this point. One night after he had performed a brilliant piano concert, many people converged around him to congratulate him. Among them was a young woman who said, "Oh sir, if only God had given me the same gift of genius that you have, I would be so happy." Beethoven replied, "Madam, it is not genius or magic. All you have to do is practice hard on your piano eight hours a day for forty years and you will be as good as I am."

There is another example from the life of Thomas Edison. He tried to create the filament in a light bulb with more than 2000 different experiments before finally finding the right one. When a young reporter asked him how it felt to fail so many times, Edison replied, "I never failed even once. Inventing the light bulb just happened to be a 2000-step process."

People like Edison and Beethoven had the right understanding about the value of hard work. That is why they were able to accomplish so much in the world. We need to have the same attitude in our lives—only then will we be able to succeed.

Amma Herself always provides us with the perfect example. Although all of Amma's actions look easy and graceful, She actually puts enormous effort into everything She does. She sings bhajans in almost 100 different languages. While She sometimes finds it difficult to pronounce the words correctly, Amma still strives to learn them, because She knows how heart-opening it is for Her children to hear Her sing bhajans in their own language.

Amma puts forth so much effort in running the hundreds of institutions that She oversees, giving direct advice about each one of them. Amma stays up every night without sleep studying all the rules and regulations in every area of management. She wants to uphold the tradition of the ancient saints and sages who, through the practice of renunciation and *tyagam*, were able to offer so much to the world. Amma says that even the breath of a Mahatma can hold the world in balance. Mother does not claim divinity, but works hard with persistence and commitment, setting the example for all of us. She says that if we have a body, then we must strive hard to make the best use of it.

Amma meets regularly with the directors of Her multi-specialty hospital (AIMS) to advise them how to properly run the hospital complex. She solves problems and gives them new ideas about implementing the day-to-day organization of the different sections of the hospital. She tells the principals of Her schools how to plan their curriculum and deals with all the problems that crop up in Her various schools. She advises the workers building houses for the poor, offering construction tips like how to implement certain new techniques in building, and how to make the bricks stronger. She explains to the carpenters certain small tricks that they had never considered, even though these people trained in their professions for years.

When we travel with Amma in India, we can see how Amma exerts Herself to give attention to the devotees who are on tour with Her. Mother may have given darshan for fifteen hours straight and may not have slept at all, but when the vehicles reach a place for a *chai* stop, She will insist on getting out of the car to be with the people traveling with Her. To always give so much more than is required is Amma's nature. Her efforts are effortless, for all Her actions flow naturally out of love. Everything She does is to teach us something or to make us happy.

On our first visit to Pondicherry, Amma had lost Her voice but still attempted to give Her usual satsang at the program. Others would have asked someone else to deliver their talk, but Amma insisted on trying to speak Herself. With Her usual sense of humor She tapped the microphone, and said in a croaky voice, "Give a little more sound," suggesting that it was not Her voice that was missing, but the volume on the microphone. The effort She put forth was overwhelming. Luckily She had warmed up by bhajan time and was able to sing. God must have overheard Her when She was joking with the mike person!

One lady who used to live in the ashram beautifully embodied Amma's teaching regarding the necessity of extending ourselves beyond expectation. This lady had two small children but nonetheless was always ready to help. When Amma's Indian tour reached Chennai that year, we had a lot of luggage that needed to be sent to America. This lady just happened to be leaving for America, so we asked if she could take something with her. She thought about it for a second and then replied, "One, two, three, four…Yes, I can actually take four suitcases for you!" You can imagine how happy I was to hear this!

Once she had taken her seat on the plane, one of the flight attendants came up to her and said, "I'm sorry madam, but we've had a bit of a problem, and we've had to upgrade you and your children to First Class." So there she was, dressed in her work outfit from the ashram, happily being led to the front of the plane. She felt a little embarrassed that her clothing was in such poor condition, but nonetheless she enjoyed the First Class service.

When the next year came around and she was visiting the ashram with her husband, she said to him, "Look dear, we really should take some luggage for them again this year." He was a little hesitant but in the end he finally agreed. This time, when they had taken their seats on the plane, the flight attendant came up to them and said, "I'm sorry, but there has been a bit of a problem and we've had to upgrade you all to Business Class." The lady turned to her husband and said, "You see? Because you were hesitant about helping out, this time we're only getting Business Class!" So never hesitate to lend a helping hand, for by exerting yourself a little more, you just might find you will be upgraded from the ordinary to the Divine.

Some people may complain that others have grace and they do not. But Amma says that the Guru's grace is like the sun, always shining on everyone. If we do not see the light, it is probably because we have kept our window shutters closed, and we must make a conscious attempt to open them. Then the light will naturally flow in, because it has always been there. If we keep the shutters closed, there is no point in blaming the sun for not giving us light. Similarly, we cannot blame the Guru for not extending grace to us—we just have to put forth the necessary resolve to open the shutters of our hearts.

Amma says that grace is behind every action that we perform, though we hardly think about it and most often take our day-to-day actions for granted. It is said that there are over three trillion cells in the body, and all function only due to grace. We may falsely believe that we are the doer, but without the grace of God, we cannot move even a muscle. One of the residents in the ashram had sprained her foot and was totally out of commission due to her injury. She came to see me and told me how this injury made her realize how great God's power

truly is. She remembered how Amma constantly reminds us that nothing can be accomplished without grace. Only after enduring difficult times and experiencing grace through healing, do we really come to understand this.

Some people say that destiny controls everything. They believe that all that happens in life is predestined, and therefore there is nothing they can do to improve their situation in life. Amma tells us that this understanding is incorrect, and that people who think in this way usually end up leaving the spiritual path. When times get difficult, instead of intensifying their spiritual efforts, they are likely to just give up and lay the blame on destiny.

Rather than despair over our fate, we should always maintain a positive attitude and persevere with good actions. As Amma points out, if we are hungry we will not say, "Let fate bring me food." If food arrives, we will not say, "Let fate put the food in my mouth." We will always take the food, put it in our mouths, and eat it. Similarly, we should not imagine that our lack of grace is the result of fate and lay the blame there. We should simply use our own will power and do all we can to align ourselves with the Divine. The effort that we put forth creates our destiny. Therefore, we should always try to make a strong, positive undertaking in everything we do.

Amma gives us the strength to face difficult situations. Our sincere efforts combined with the Guru's grace can overcome any negative circumstances.

A long-time European devotee once told me a moving story from Amma's visit to Europe earlier in the year. His wife had seen Amma wearing an orange sari during an earlier Devi Bhava and she had been overcome with the beauty of it. In Munich, she saw that the sari was for sale and told her husband that he had to buy it for her. He was overwhelmed with the thought of how much it was going to cost him! But he went to buy it for her anyway, and was asked, "Do you want the blouse also?" He did not know so he went back to ask his wife. Of course she wanted the blouse too. When it was mentioned to Amma that she wanted to buy the sari, Amma said she could have it on one condition only, that she had to wear it. This woman was devastated at the thought, but finally agreed. She put on the blouse and sari and got ready to go for darshan with her husband. When they approached Amma, She made a big fuss about the woman and told her how beautiful she looked. Then Amma said, "I am going to marry you both!" The husband was shocked because he said he was already married to his wife. Yet Amma insisted on doing the ceremony again for them.

About six months later, his wife died suddenly of a heart attack. As he held her in his arms and felt she had no pulse, he said to her, "Go! Don't stay with me!" He motioned for her spirit to be free and travel up. Knowing the nature of the body is ever changing and that the Atman is everlasting, he knew it was time for her to go and did not want to hold her spirit back. When he told this story to me, I was struck by how amazing it was that he could detach himself from her at that time, that he could do the right thing and let his wife go.

He said that now Amma's love fills the gap that had previously been filled by his wife's presence. It was truly Mother's grace that he remembered the teachings of impermanence at exactly the right time. The devotee really felt that with Amma performing the marriage ceremony earlier in the year, and with his wife wearing orange, that She had given his wife sannyas before she had died. Amma later told the man that his wife would not have to be reborn, as she had merged with the *Paramatman*. It was so moving to hear him tell these stories—and to see the surrender in him that brought him peace through his wife's death.

When terrible things happen in the world, some will blame God for His cruelty. We should remember that suffering arises not due to any cruelty of God but because of our previous actions. Everything happens according to the law of karma. Amma says that life consists of only two events: performing an action and experiencing the results of that action. If we have performed wrong actions in the past, we can gloomily sit back and experience what is due to come as a result of those actions. Or we can try to perform good actions now, so that our future will be brighter.

Amma says again and again "*kripa rakshikatte,*" or "may grace save us." Only grace will save us. She knows that behind everything lies grace. People all over the world have experienced Amma's grace. Diseases have been healed. Many have been saved from accidents and even early death. The grace of the Guru is so strong that it will finally work the ultimate miracle in each of us. The impossible becomes possible only through the Guru's grace. That grace is our only refuge, and it is the only refuge we need.

With Thy bewitching form,
My heart ever belongs to Thee.
What am I to do who am torn between two worlds?

Can You not cut asunder this wretched fetter
That holds me away from You?
I desire not liberation nor immortality,
This You may give to others.

I long only to become lost in Thee,
Drunk with the bliss of seeing Thy form before me always.
Never will my eyes tire of drinking in Your beauty,
Ever new in splendour and love, as each second goes by.

Take this dream and make it a reality,
For what else was my birth meant?
This I know to be the truth.

Chapter 11

Selflessness and Humility

*"You are the ones who have to soar high
into the vast sky of spirituality.
And to do that,
you need the wings of selflessness and love.
The opportunity to love and serve others
should be considered a rare gift,
a blessing from God."*

Amma

There is a story from the Buddhist tradition that beautifully illustrates the power of selflessness. Once there was a king who had three sons, the youngest being an especially loving and compassionate little boy. One day the king and his family went on a picnic, and soon after arriving, the princes ran off to play in the woods. After going deep into the forest, they were thrilled to come across a tigress that had just given birth. Extremely exhausted with hunger, it appeared that she was on the verge of eating her newborn cubs.

The young boy asked his brothers, "What would the tigress need to eat in order to revive?"

"Fresh meat or blood," they replied. "But where can that be found?" he asked. "Is there anyone who would give his own flesh and blood to feed her, and save the lives of her and her babies?" His brothers shrugged and gave no reply.

Deeply moved by the plight of the tigress and her cubs, the young boy began to think, "For so long I have wandered uselessly through the cycle of birth and death, life after life. And because of my desires, anger and ignorance, I have done very little to help other beings. Here at last is a great opportunity."

He told his other brothers to go on ahead, saying he would catch up with them later. Quietly he crept back to the tigress and lay down on the ground in front of her, offering himself as food. The tigress was so weak that she could not even open her mouth, so the boy found a sharp stick and cut a deep gash in his own body. The blood flowed out, and the tigress licked it, and with this she grew strong enough to open her jaws and eat him. Through this extraordinary act of self-sacrifice, the boy succeeded in saving the lives of the tigress and her cubs.

According to the story, which is considered to be true by many Buddhists, the boy was then born again, and through the merit of his compassionate action he progressed rapidly towards enlightenment and finally took birth as Lord Buddha.

The story does not end there. The boy's selfless action did more than accelerate his own spiritual progress; it also purified the tigress and her cubs of their karma, and even removed any karmic debt they might have owed him for saving their lives. His compassionate sacrifice was so strong that it created a beneficial karmic link between them that continued far into the future.

The tigress and her cubs were eventually reborn as the Buddha's first five disciples, the very first souls to receive his teachings after his enlightenment.

Such is the power of selfless action. Amma is always trying to teach us how to live selflessly. Just as the candle melts itself down to nothing in order to give light to others, and the incense stick burns itself to ash to offer its fragrance to everyone, Amma wants us to completely offer our lives in service to the world.

Of course, She doesn't actually recommend that we climb over the fence of the lion cage at the zoo! That kind of sacrifice is not really necessary these days. Daily life gives us plenty of opportunities to sacrifice our egos in the service of others.

Becoming more selfless does not really take so much effort. We just have to start putting other people before ourselves, and try to always be helpful in whatever way we can. If we just practice those basic steps, we will be well on our way to selflessness. Spiritual life does not mean that one must chant perfect Sanskrit mantras or be able to sit in the lotus position for hours on end without moving. The whole basis of a successful spiritual life is really just becoming simpler, kinder, and more helpful. If we try to become decent human beings and cultivate these basic down-to-earth qualities in our daily lives, then automatically all the great qualities will follow.

Whether you are a householder or live in an ashram, selflessness is a quality that needs to be developed on the spiritual path. Married people with families are very fortunate, for they will naturally have plenty of opportunities to develop selflessness in their family lives. If they want to find happiness in their home life, they will have to learn to think of others before themselves. If a mother has a child, then she will always have to think of the child first. Even if the mother is sick, she will still forego her own food or rest to care for her child. House-holders automatically receive special training in developing selflessness. They should simply bring the lessons they have learned to their spiritual life.

One of Amma's brahmacharis had a moving experience that reveals the qualities of a selfless mother. While he was traveling on a train, a woman followed by her nine children came into his compartment and sat down. They were obviously very poor, and she looked hungry. Since he was carrying extra food, he gave her some of it. She distributed everything to her children and kept nothing for herself. Nonetheless she seemed happy because all her children had received some food. Then he noticed that the small baby in her lap was looking up at her with a lot of love. The baby was holding a piece of food in its hand, and suddenly it reached up and put the food into the mother's mouth. The brahmachari felt he was seeing the hand of God feeding that mother, through her own baby. When we develop this kind of selfless love, God will always look after us.

At first, most people come to Amma in order to get love from Her, and they receive many hugs and kisses. Eventually, most devotees discover that more of Her love and grace flows to us when we decide we want to become givers instead of takers. Real happiness is the outcome of selflessness. It is a cosmic law that the more we give to others the more we will receive. We only find true peace of mind when we think of others before ourselves. If we do this, so much more joy will flow our way.

Everyone longs for happiness in life. If we can stop try-ing to find pleasure and enjoyment for ourselves and think instead, "What can I do for others?" then true happiness will dawn. It is only when we ask for nothing in return for our service that we receive the real joy. Even when we understand spiritual principles, as long as we are focused only on ourselves it is difficult to find happiness. So we should train ourselves to experience happiness by bringing joy to others.

A few years ago a Special Olympic Games was held in Seattle. The participants were all children who were either physically or mentally disabled. At one of the events, nine children were assembled for a 100-yard race. When the race began, all nine began running towards the finish line. About half way, one boy tripped and fell. He started to cry. The other eight racers heard him crying and slowed down. One by one, they stopped, turned around, and went back to help him. A girl with Down's syndrome bent over and kissed him saying, "This will make it better." Then they all linked arms and walked together to the finish line. Everyone in the stadium leapt to their feet, and the cheering continued for ten minutes.

Instead of trying to find love, we should try to give love. If we look for others to give us love, we will always be unhappy. But if we allow ourselves to be as loving as we can with everyone, we will instantly feel happier. Instead of looking for what we can take from the world, if we start asking, "What can I offer the world?" then we will start to become like Amma. For this is how She leads Her life. She is the perfect example of selflessness. Love flows from Her like a river, because She is the source, She is love itself. She is not trying to take love from anyone, for She is ever full; and because She is always giving love, we cannot help but love Her.

When we look at Amma during darshan, we can see Her bubbling over with effervescent joy. While giving darshan, She will be saying things like, "Make sure the old people are brought first. See that everyone is given water to drink. There is an old man in the hall who needs help in coming up." She

will always be looking after all the people's needs and will be aware of everything happening in the hall. Amma is aware of everything around Her, in every direction, 360 degrees. In contrast, look at us—we can barely consider what is right in front of us. If we are thinking of anyone, it is most often only of ourselves. Amma is always thinking of everyone else but Herself.

Another extremely considerate person is the President of India, Dr. A.P.J. Abdul Kalam. Amma was invited to visit him at Rashtrapati Bhavan, the Presidential Mansion in New Delhi, and there were several of us in the room with him. Even though he was talking primarily to Amma, he still had the consideration to look at everyone else. His awareness was there with everyone, not only with Amma. He made us all feel like honored guests.

On another occasion, Amma went to visit President Kalam. Amma got out of the car without Her shoes, and I left them behind thinking She would not need them. The President greeted Amma and after talking with Her for a while, invited Her to walk in the beautiful gardens that surround the property. We were alarmed to think that She would walk with bare feet, but Amma insisted that She had been raised in a village and was quite used to walking barefoot. The President, in turn, replied that he would not wear his shoes either, exclaiming, "Amma, I grew up in a village too!" Watching them walk barefoot together through the flowers and trees, I was reminded of the importance of remaining simple no matter how great one becomes.

We should all aspire to develop such humility. If we strive in that direction, we can learn to be courteous and kind in our behavior and become more aware of other people's needs. We should always try to take into account the feelings of others and carefully consider how our actions will affect them.

It is often said that the humility of the Guru will be so great that it will be hard to distinguish the Guru from the disciple. With Amma, this is certainly the case. In August 2000, we attended the Millennium World Peace Summit of Religious and Spiritual Leaders at the United Nations in New York City. It was quite a long affair consisting of two days of listening to different speeches. Amma's speech was on the second day and afterwards we were happy our obligations were finished. After having fasted all day, we looked forward to returning to the luxurious hotel room provided for us. Well, I was looking forward to it. The Swamis had all left the main auditorium and only Amma and I sat among the crowd, listening to the remaining speeches.

Knowing how gracious Amma is and thinking that She would not initiate leaving, I came up with a plan for our escape. I stood up, hoping Amma would be a good obedient Guru and simply follow me. But as I stood up, Amma remained seated, intent on listening to the speeches. She clapped when everyone else clapped and seemed to find all the talks in English and other languages that we could not even understand terribly interesting. She totally ignored me.

I tried a second time, standing up saying, "Come on Amma, we can go now!" Again She ignored me. I thought, "Well if I *really* walk out into the aisle, then Amma will *have* to follow me." So I picked up my bag and made my way out into the aisle, ready to go. Amma remained enthralled listening to the speech, which was in Korean, I think, at that time. She continued to ignore me. She knew the correct thing to do was to listen to the speech, even if we did not understand it.

I surrendered to looking like an idiot after standing up and down so many times and just sat down on my bag in the aisle waiting for Amma to decide when to leave. Eventually, when one of the talks finished, and Amma believed the time was appropriate, She graciously stood up and made Her way out. And, as it should have been, I followed.

Another revealing incident occurred when we were traveling through Washington, D.C. In America, airport security had become extremely strict, and sometimes people were randomly selected for an extra security check. On this particular day Amma was chosen for the additional search, and I accompanied Her to translate.

The security officer was a strong-looking woman with an abrupt manner. Amma had taken a seat, and the officer told Her to stand up. I can speak a little Malayalam, but I am not really fluent, so I was searching in my mind for how to say "stand up" politely. However, what came out of my mouth was the word "*Erenekke*," something I have often heard said, which literally means, "Get up!" Amma obediently stood up. Then it occurred to me, "Oh my goodness, I think I was just very rude to Amma," since this term is usually only used for talking to youngsters and is not something that should be said to the Guru. But Amma was not upset, for She has no ego to be offended.

The security officer then ordered Amma to stand on one leg with Her two arms out in the air in a ballet pose. I was trying to think of how to say "ballet pose" in Malayalam and wondering if Amma would even know what ballet was. So I settled for telling Her to stand in a yoga position. Amma graciously obliged. As the lady was waving her metal detector over Amma's body, her manner softened. "She's just *soooo* beautiful!" the officer exclaimed. Everywhere we go, people realize there is something very special about this simple woman dressed in white.

The rest of the group traveling with Amma was watching from a distance, receiving the teaching in humility She was giving them. Anyone else in Her situation might have said, "Don't you know how important I am?" But Amma just smiled kindly and patiently allowed this woman to have Her darshan in this way. Once again Amma demonstrated through Her personal example the divine qualities that we should all try to imbibe.

Amma advises that whenever we feel our ego rising up and claiming importance, we should just look at the vast sky or the deep blue sea, and see how insignificant we are in comparison. Real greatness is measured by humility. Instead of trying to make ourselves feel bigger, we should try to become aware of just how small we really are in the infinite universe. Amma says that when we feel smaller than an ant, we become bigger than all of creation.

We human beings tend to believe that our species occupies the highest rung on the ladder of creation, but we can learn a lot of lessons from Mother Nature. Trees can teach us a great deal about selflessness. The coconut tree, for example, offers every part of itself to us. The flesh of the coconut is food and the coconut milk is a nourishing drink. In India, the husk and leaves become firewood, and rope is made from the fibers. The coconut leaves are woven into mats, used to thatch houses, or made into brooms. The wood is used to build houses and make fences. The tree gives its life force to us totally, not expecting anything in return, and will do so even if we carve our initials in its bark or try to chop it down. Such selfless love puts our own lives to shame.

The earth goes through so much trouble to support us, without complaining at all. Just consider one plate of rice with spinach, dhal and vegetables. How many nutrients were required from the earth to grow that rice, and how much toil and effort did it take to cultivate and thresh it? How many drops of precious rain and golden rays of sunshine were needed to grow the vegetables? How much energy did it take for a cow to eat grass, which had grown for weeks, and then to miraculously turn it into milk that becomes our curd? The universe gives so much for us for just one meal that we consume in a few minutes! Do we ever contemplate this?

Like Mother Nature, Amma is sacrificing Herself to teach us how to lead our lives correctly and how to serve the world selflessly. Amma's life has always been one of only giving, never of taking, apart from taking the pain and suffering of those who offer their sorrows to Her.

The poet Hafiz wrote,

> *"The sun never says to the earth,*
> *'You owe me.'*
> *Look what happens with a love like that.*
> *It lights up the whole sky."*

Amma is giving the world and us so much joy. If we keep giving to the world, it will look after us. Examples of this can be readily seen in Amma's life. When She was young, She slept outside on the bare ground or soaked in the mud of the backwaters that surrounded Her family's house. Sometimes months would go by when Amma would survive by taking just a few *tulasi* leaves. She never looked for food but Mother Nature provided for Her. Animals would bring Her sustenance.

An eagle would drop fish in Her lap; a dog would bring Her food packets in its mouth; and a cow would come up to Her so that She could drink milk directly from its udder. Amma said that when She spent hours crying to God, parrots would come and sit and shed tears along with Her. All of nature joined with Her in the quest for union with the Divine. Such was the compassion of the animals, in stark contrast to Amma's own family who thought She was crazy. Even today we occasionally find strange offerings on the steps leading to Amma's room or on the doormat outside Her door. Amma says that animals leave these gifts for Her.

While nature always gives, it is unfortunately the disposition of human beings always to take, asking for more, but not giving back much in return. We owe such a huge karmic debt to nature, to the world, to the suffering people everywhere. The only way to repay it is to try our best to learn from Amma, who is doing so much to uplift everyone.

What is needed is for us to become free from our selfish egos. In today's world, selfless workers are needed to uplift humanity from its suffering. Mere talk of performing good actions is not enough. We must follow Amma's example and put our words into action for our own peace of mind as much as for the world.

Amma's life is the perfect example of selflessness. We cannot exactly follow in Her footsteps, but we can at least try to absorb a fraction of the selflessness and perfect love that overflows from Her. If we do so, then surely we too will one day become a blessing to the world.

One cannot say that Amma's health has ever really been good. People often beg Her to try to heal Herself. Amma's reply is that She has given Herself as an offering to the world.

A gift once given should never be taken back. Although She has healed so many others, Amma will never show any concern for Her own welfare. Her prayer has always been, "Let me take my last breath while consoling someone on my shoulder." And surely this will come to pass.

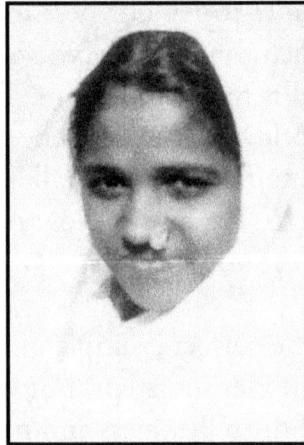

*I offer all to You
But my mind, like a traitor,
Steals back to the world.*

*My heart cries for You,
But the world pulls me away.
What a wretched birth is this.*

*Before I found You,
I committed so many sins.
Now I long to hold onto Your lotus feet
But my sins pull me away.*

*I want to drown in Your ocean of mercy,
But I drown in my own tears.
Maya has such a strong hold on me,
Please make her let go!*

Chapter 12

❈

Renunciation

*"Behind every good cause,
you will find somebody
who has renounced everything
and dedicated their life to it."*

Amma

I once asked Amma, "What is real vairagya (detachment)?
"Amma's answer was, "Holding your nose when a foul stench
may come." I was shocked by Her answer, as I would have
thought the opposite. She seemed to be saying that we should
not take in a foul stench, thinking to ourselves the whole time,
"I am so great; I can put up with this wretched smell." In fact,
She was saying that we should have the discrimination to hold
our nose to avoid taking in a foul stench. Amma was teaching me that true vairagya gives us the knowledge to perform
the right action, in the right place, at the right time. But how
many of us have this detachment? Most of us travel through
life swayed by desires and attachments.

Peace comes and goes; it never remains with us permanently because of our likes and dislikes. The cause of all our
suffering is the desires within the mind. Therefore, we should

try to remain detached by keeping our mind away from the things that it wants to rush into. Only when we transcend all our desires completely, can we really be happy and peaceful at all times. Amma has succeeded in doing this, and through the power of Her complete Self-mastery, She has been able to accomplish extraordinary things and render great service to humanity.

Amma shows us that the real source of happiness lies waiting for us, not in the world, but in ourselves. If we can practice renunciation, we will be able to live in the world, even to love the world, but not mistakenly think that the objects of the world will bring us peace of mind or satisfaction. In realizing this truth, we can turn our journey inward and hopefully find peace of mind within.

Mother's life is a perfect example of true renunciation, always providing us with lessons to learn. One year when we arrived at the Bangalore ashram, we found that a nice new room had been built for Amma. We started up the stairs to the room, but when Amma saw the green marble that was used on the stairway, She became quite angry and sat down halfway up the stairs. She would not even look at the room. After seeing how fancy the stairway was, She imagined that the room was even more extravagant. Even in India, marble is expensive. She was irate at the thought that so much money that could have been spent on the poor had been wasted to create a nice room for Her that She would only use for two days every year.

Amma has said that, as spiritual people, we should not think about our own comfort. Instead, we should learn to flow like a river. If some obstacle like the root of a tree obstructs the path, the river gently flows around it. Like the river's ability to change its flow, we should learn to adjust to challenges and obstacles in life. By adapting to uncomfortable situations, we train ourselves to be happy with whatever God provides, trusting that whatever we truly need and deserve will come to us unasked. When we travel, Amma instructs us not to ask people to go out of their way for us, nor should we bother our host with any extra personal requests. We should not create more difficulties for others and should be satisfied with what we receive.

When we travel with Amma on the World Tours, there are often nights without sleep, as we travel to different cities or countries every few days after long all-night programs. Sometimes we do not even have time to eat or drink anything all day. People coming to see Amma observe what we have to go through with all the hard work and lack of sleep and can never understand how we do it. It is only out of our love for Amma that we are able to keep up with this rigorous schedule. Love gives us the strength to accomplish anything in life.

At *Amritavarsham50*, apart from hundreds of thousands of Indian devotees, over 3000 people came from different foreign countries to attend the four days of conferences and cultural events in honor of Amma's 50th birthday. For many of them it was their first visit to India, and some found the conditions challenging; but one would never have known it from the look on people's faces. Everyone was beaming with joy. Many of us hardly ate or slept for days, yet it was the highlight of our lives. Out of their love for Amma, people were able to sit in the intense heat and burning sun for hours and were happy to sacrifice the comforts of their everyday life in order to attend this special event. When we think of how we celebrate our own birthday, we think of receiving gifts and being treated in a special way. But for Amma, it was an opportunity to bring everyone together to pray for peace and harmony in the world.

Some people fall so much in love with Amma that they follow Her all around the world, giving up everything to follow the "stealer of hearts." Many westerners have even come to live with Her permanently in India. As the years have gone by, Amma has totally transformed the lives of Her devotees. They may have had well-paid jobs and a luxurious lifestyle, but this lifestyle became meaningless in comparison with the peace of mind found by living a simple life at the feet of a Mahatma. Likewise, many of the devotees who still live away from Amma have chosen to give their time and talents in selfless service, taking part in Amma's charitable activities in various locations around the world. I have seen with my own eyes that these people have been changed for the better by imbibing Amma's teachings and putting them into practice in their lives.

During the 2003 South India tour, we visited the city of Rameshwaram. A large crowd was waiting to receive Amma's darshan—there must have been at least 20,000 people. The darshan continued through the night and well into the next day. After the program finally finished in the late morning, Amma unexpectedly chose to travel towards the next evening's program site in the car, instead of the other vehicle She usually rides in. She had not eaten or slept since early the previous day, which was always a difficult experience for us, but nothing new for Amma. As we were driving, Amma mentioned that She was a little hungry, so we searched for something to eat, but the food that had been prepared for Her was in the other vehicle, and Amma said She did not want us to stop to get it.

After some time we paused at a railway crossing, and a young boy appeared with some strange-looking kind of root vegetable. Amma was curious to know what it was, so the driver found two rupees in his pocket and purchased two pieces of the vegetable. It was half-cooked, very fibrous and slightly bitter; but after a taste, Amma decided that this would be Her meal for the day. She offered us a little as prasad and chewed on the rest of it.

Even after staying up all night, still Amma never yearned for a bed to lay Her head on, but was content to sit in the car. After not eating for more than twenty-four hours, She was happy to have what two rupees could buy as Her meal. Amma can be happy under any circumstance because Her source of joy comes not from the external world but from the internal world.

Expecting peace and happiness from the external world is like digging a hole in the desert hoping to find water to quench our thirst. Even if we dig for years, we will probably never find water. If by some miracle we happen to discover some, it will most likely be salt-water, which will only increase our thirst. In coming to Amma our thirst is satisfied, for She teaches us to find true contentment within.

Once there was a rich man who hoarded all his money and spent it only on luxuries. One day, when he was opening the door of his Mercedes Benz, a truck came speeding by and hit it, ripping the door off its hinges. A policeman arrived and found the man fuming with rage, complaining bitterly about the damage to his precious car.

"Are you crazy?" the policeman asked. "You're so worried about your beautiful car that you didn't notice your left arm was ripped off!"

"Oh NO!" said the man, looking down and noticing that his arm was missing, "Where's my ROLEX?"

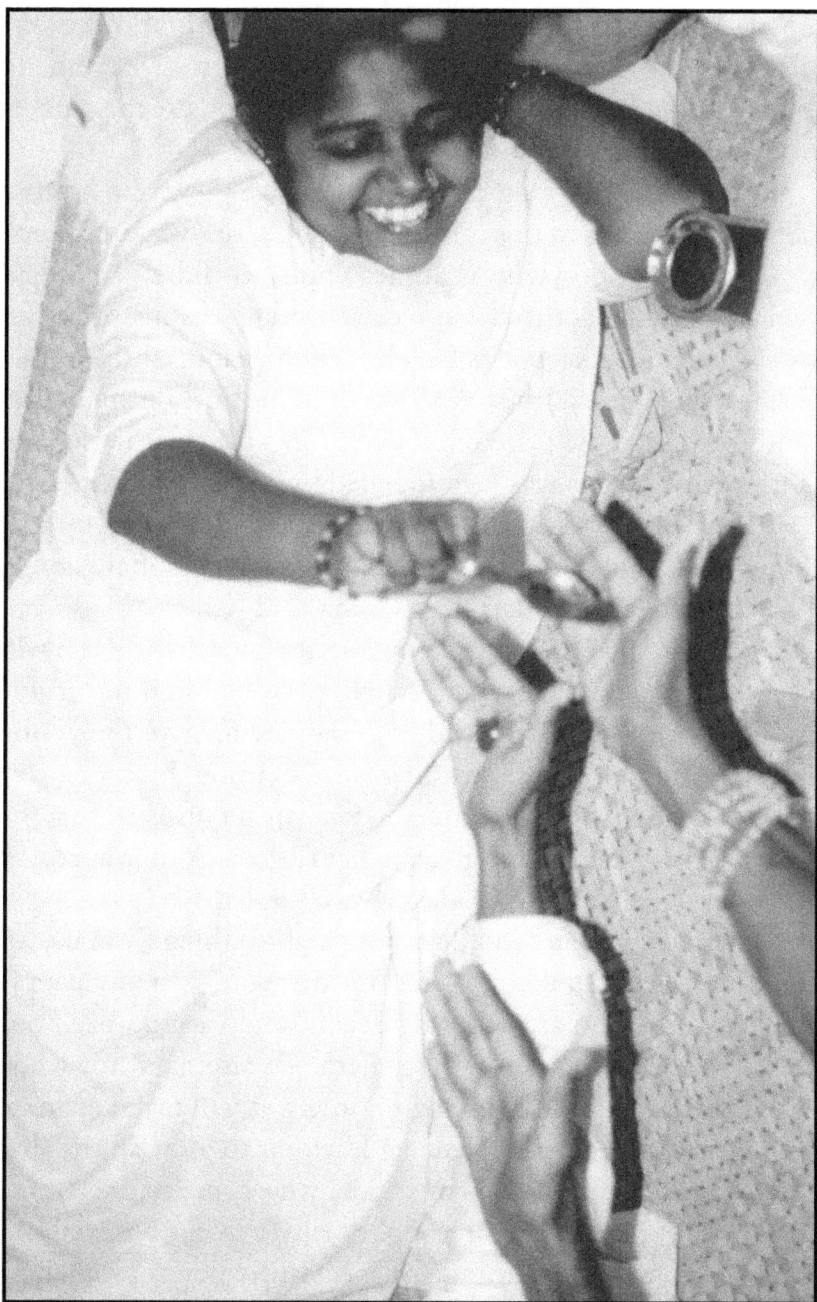

When we understand that happiness is not found in external objects or sensory pleasures, then surely we will want to stop wasting money on unnecessary things and use this money to serve the poor instead.

Many of the young children who have grown up around Amma have learned this important lesson. This year in Europe a young Swiss boy who is an accomplished flute player had won a national contest. He received money as his prize but was reluctant to keep it as he felt it really belonged to Amma. He felt that She was the one that played the flute through him, and he wanted the prize money to be given to Her to be used for charity. Amma was very touched by his thoughtfulness.

While happy for her brother's success, the boy's younger sister was sad because she felt she had nothing to offer Amma. When she went for darshan, Amma told her, "You also can learn how to play an instrument, and then maybe you can win a prize and give the money to help poor children too." One week later on her birthday, her grandparents gave the young girl some money for ice cream. Instead of using this money for her own enjoyment, she came for darshan and insisted that she wanted this money to be given to help others. Amma accepted the offering, and the girl's desire was fulfilled.

Amma says that God does not need anything from us, for God is ever full and complete. But there are so many people in the world who are suffering deeply, and they do need our help. In the process of serving them, we also gain, for when we have the attitude of giving to others, it will make us more expansive and compassionate and help us to grow spiritually.

Out of the thousands of people who come to see Amma every day in India, maybe only twenty percent are well off, and not in need of anything. The next thirty percent somehow manage to have enough for their basic needs, but nothing more. The remaining fifty percent are really struggling to survive. Often these people will forego food, medical care and other necessities of life because they are so very poor. To come and see Amma they may have had to borrow other people's clothes because they did not have anything decent to wear. Sometimes women have to sell their bangles or earrings to get enough money to travel to the ashram. Some people will even go without food for a day or two in order to save up the money to be able to come to see Amma.

Recently, while we were in Singapore, a reporter asked Amma what Her opinion was on the source of all the problems in the world. Amma replied that She thought that poverty was the greatest enemy of society. She said it is one of the primary reasons that people become terrorists, or turn to drugs, or commit murders. It is due to poverty that people resort to theft and prostitution, just to be able to find the means to survive. Amma has said that if we eradicate poverty, then many of the prevailing social evils will be cleared away.

Since we all have to work for our livelihood in one way or another, Amma suggests that everyone should work an extra half hour a day for the poor, as a service to the world. She says that if each of us gives up a small portion of our daily earnings to charities that serve the poor, then eighty percent of all the problems in the world could be eliminated.

It is said that human beings have two major problems. One comes when our desires do not get fulfilled, and the other comes when they do. It is also said that when God wants to punish us, He gives us everything we ask for. We often pray for many things, but once we have them, we realize we did not really want them after all. Some people spend their entire lives worrying about their health or chasing after name, fame and possessions. People who run after these things will rarely attain them, and if by some chance they do, they will neither be happy for long nor experience any real peace of mind. It is better to let things run after us, than for us to pursue them. What we truly need, will surely be given by God.

Some people have all the luxuries in the world but are still miserable. There are even people living in palatial air-conditioned homes who end up committing suicide. We rarely hear of people regretting not having had more possessions or more money as they lie on their deathbed. Instead, we hear of people regretting not having enjoyed life more and not having learned how to truly love others.

When faced with death, everything we craved for in life may suddenly seem unimportant. Amma says we try to insure our lives, thinking that wealth will serve as security against the unknown, but we forget that death can overpower us at any moment. Remembering this truth, we must try to lead a righteous life. Our lives should not be like that of a dog that barks at its own reflection in a mirror, taking it to be real. We should not chase after shadows, but should turn within to find true contentment. When we indulge in sense pleasures, we are wasting our precious life energy. A dog that chews on a bone may taste its own blood and relish the flavor, thinking that it is coming from the bone. This is what our search for happiness in the external world is like. What we believe to be the source of our happiness is actually an illusion that leads to suffering.

Nothing in this world is eternal. When we are attached to external objects, there can be no other possible result but sorrow. The lesson that sorrow gives us is that we should turn to God instead. Amma says, "Renunciation is only possible when there is love for the higher goal of God." We cannot force renunciation—we can only try to develop the good qualities, and the bad ones will naturally just fall away.

🪷

Take away these chains that bind me.
My heart longs only to ceaselessly love You
But my mind, like a traitor,
Drifts back to the world.
I am helplessly caught
Between the sorrow of delusion and sweet bliss
Derived from seeking Your merciful form.
How many more days
Of agony must I bear,
Before You offer me the touch
Of Your lotus feet?
For how long will this frail form endure
The torture of separation from You?

🪷

Chapter 13

✿

Attitude is What Matters Most

"Acquire more strength to confront the impediments
that might arise in your spiritual path.
We cannot change situations in life,
but we can change our attitude towards them."

Amma

We can control very little in our lives. We cannot control the actions of others, nor can we control the outcome of our own actions. The attitude with which we perform an action is the only thing that we *do* have complete control over in life. Amma says that we have no control over the wind that blows over the ocean, but if we align our sails with the direction of the wind, it will surely take us ahead.

Life is a mixture of pleasure and pain—it is never without anguish and sorrow. Only when we transcend the desires within us can we really be happy and peaceful at all times. If someone praises us one day and the next day criticizes us, we may become upset. Amma says that we should develop a mind that will not be affected by these changing circumstances. As spiritual seekers, we must learn to have equanimity and evenness of mind in all situations in life.

If we consider the circumstances of Amma's life and how She has dealt with them over the years, we can see the truth that how we respond to situations in life really determines our inner experience. Although She was not always so well accepted, today Amma is renowned for Her vast humanitarian activities and Her simple acts of love demonstrated through the daily darshans. Even in the face of adversity and contempt, Amma has never been disturbed.

Many years ago, some villagers who lived near the ashram were very much against Amma. They did not understand Amma or anything about spirituality at all, so they were often very critical of Her and the ashram. In time, they came to understand more of Amma's greatness.

In early September of 2000, we returned to India after Amma had delivered a speech at the United Nations General Assembly in New York. People were so proud of Her as She had become the first woman to speak in Malayalam at the U.N. For many miles leading up to the ashram, all the houses had lit oil lamps in front of them in honor of Amma. People that had once reviled Her, were now revering Her. Still She remained unaffected. Once the villagers threw stones at Her—now they throw flowers.

One day one of the girls in the ashram began telling me how overwhelmed by sorrow she was. She said that she felt so far away from Amma and that she had no relationship with Her. Amma then gave her some advice, "You can look up at the sun and think, 'I want to be like the sun!' But you know practically that this can never really happen. At least why not try to become like a firefly? It is enough to be like a firefly. We might not be able to shine that full light and warmth onto the world like the sun, but at least we can become like a tiny glow in the dark. A small beacon of light to guide someone's way."

Sorrows are a part of life. They are just like birds flying in the sky. We should just allow them to fly; we should not allow them to build a nest on our heads. We should neither brood over sorrows, nor allow them to be with us forever. Instead, we should set them free. We may feel that we are in darkness, but in truth that darkness does not really exist. Amma says, "Open your hearts and you will find that there has never been any darkness, there has only been light. If we feel the darkness, we should remember that it carries in its womb the light of dawn." Amma reminds us again and again that we are the light of God, and that light is always there within us. We simply close our doors and windows, and then complain that the light does not shine in.

Our attitude determines our experience of life, and whether we experience sorrow and pain or happiness. Most of the time we tend to dwell too much on the problems and difficulties we have, instead of remembering all the good things that have been given to us. There are so many people who are troubled by major problems and sorrows. If we remember how much we truly have, especially having had the grace to meet Amma, our experience of life will seem like night and day in comparison.

A lady from New Zealand told me of how one day Amma taught her an important lesson. She was trying to finish wiping down the tables and cleaning up in the ashram canteen after everyone had eaten. Suffering from arthritis, she felt annoyed at the prospect of still having to work a little longer with a nagging pain in her hip. Along came one of the young girls who lived in the ashram. She was nine years old and very sweet. Just recently she had broken her wrist in a fall and had a plaster cast put on her right arm. The girl very cheerfully walked up to the lady and asked her if she could help. The lady looked at her cast and remarked that she had hurt her arm, hadn't she? "Well, I still have one good arm left to help with!" the child smilingly replied. This lady felt completely humbled. Here was a young child that had problems as great as her own, but still she had the desire to help others.

Nowadays few people approach selfless service with real love and joy. Amma many times has mentioned that people do work a lot in the ashram, but not always with the right outlook. It has been jokingly said that at first some girls come to the ashram with a helpful frame of mind. They take a broom and start sweeping. But after a while their helpful nature disappears and instead of using the broom to sweep, they run around hitting people on the head with it!

When we see people who do their work with real love and concentration, then we also start to share their joy. It becomes contagious. For example, people have told me that they really feel the love the brahmacharinis have for Amma come shining through when they have *ayurvedic* massage in the ashram's *Panchakarma* clinic. Giving a massage may not seem like a spiritual practice, but anything, when done with the right attitude, can become a vehicle for us to receive Amma's grace.

The intention behind an action is most important and ultimately determines the result. A murderer may use a knife to kill and will suffer negative karma because of his evil intention. On the other hand, a doctor may perform a surgical operation with a knife with the intention of saving a patient's life. This intent will result in positive karma. Although the instrument and the action are the same, the attitude behind the action is different.

Since the attitude determines the result, we should try to perform our actions with a good attitude so that God's grace can flow to us.

According to Amma, the definition of spirituality is that it is an art that teaches us how to live our entire life in perfection. An understanding of spiritual principles is the most important type of knowledge that we can possess in life, for spirituality teaches us the way to live in this materialistic world and how to manage our lives. Even if we have faith in God, our attachments can still take our energy away if we do not have the right understanding. A person can lead a happy life if they understand spiritual principles and know that the nature of the world is unreal and forever changing. However, someone not aware of the inevitable ups and downs in life will always find sorrow, fear and anxiety.

Obstacles can make us stronger. The beautiful rainbow with its brilliant spectrum of colors only appears when there is rain. Similarly, happiness and sorrow are like two sides of a coin. Through something bad, something good can also happen. For example, in 2001 in Gujarat, the large earthquake created an incredible amount of suffering for the people affected, but it also aroused intense compassion in the hearts of people all over the world who wanted to help.

I remember being touched by an article I had read about a group of Gujarati porters in one of the railway stations and their compassionate response to the devastation from the earthquake. Porters are often perceived as being callous, as they make their living by harassing passengers and overcharging them for carrying their bags. However, this group of porters was different. In the aftermath of the earthquake they pooled their money, cooked some food, and served free meals to those

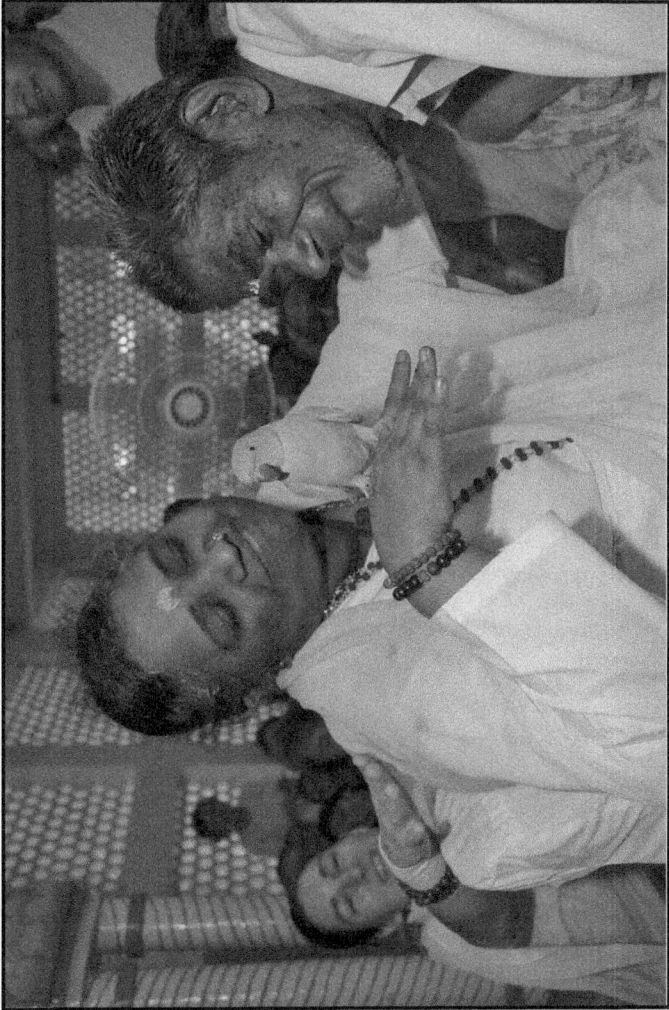

who arrived in the railway station. They opened their hearts, caring for those who were suffering instead of worrying about their own personal gain.

Many of the Gujarati people had lost their homes and their loved ones in the earthquake. When the affected devotees came for Amma's darshan in Ahmedabad, She was most concerned about them and their well-being. She asked them, "How are you managing? Can you cope with this great loss?" They answered Her quite calmly, "God had given to us and God has taken away." They were not as distraught as we had imagined they would be, but were accepting of their situation.

Amma reminds us that the days are quickly passing. We can either laugh or cry, so is it not better to laugh, to maintain a positive perspective no matter what life presents us? While we were in Canada I read a newspaper article about some fires that had occurred in a farmland area. One potato farmer who was over eighty years old had his whole farmland and ancestral home totally burned to ashes. He had nothing left at all except the clothes he wore. Everything had been burnt to a crisp. When reporters asked him how he felt about losing everything, his reply was, "Well, I think I'm the first farmer in history who has had his spuds cooked before they were even harvested!" The reporter was amazed that he could joke about such a great loss and asked him, "How can you joke about losing everything?" His reply was, "Well, laugh or cry, days are flying by, it's not for us to wonder why." This is the approach we should all bring to our spiritual lives.

Each of us can choose our attitude towards situations in life. If we try hard enough, we can almost always find something positive, even in what may seem like the worst possible scenario. In the concentration camps that existed in Germany during

World War II, there were some men who were remembered for walking through the dilapidated huts comforting others and offering them their last piece of bread. There were not many of these generous souls, but they will always be remembered. Even though everything had been taken away from them, these few men chose to give right up until the end when they had nothing left. Through giving, they were able to experience the joy of life.

It is important to have a positive state of mind. We must have innocence, sincerity and total faith. If we have a half-hearted attitude, we will never be able to reach the goal.

There is a funny story about a woman and her two young boys. The boys wanted to see a particular movie. They pleaded with their mom saying, "But there is only a *little bit* of violence and a *little bit* of sex." She thought about it and decided to teach them a lesson about what a little bit of something could do. So she baked some brownies and said to them, "I made these brownies, and I put just a *little bit* of dog poop in them, but you won't even taste it. You won't even know it's there. And if you eat one of these, then you can go and see the movie." They were so disgusted by this that they would not even touch the brownies. This story illustrates how just a little bit of negativity, selfishness or insincerity can make a lot of difference.

If we have an open heart and make the right amount of effort, God's grace will come to us. One year, during the Devi Bhava in Japan, a man in the audience sang *Ishwara Tumhi* in Japanese. Amma was surprised to hear him sing this bhajan. Someone explained to Amma that for twenty-six years this man had worked six days a week at his family's Chinese restaurant. For all these years he had only one day off a week, always on a Wednesday. Although he was a devotee of Amma for many years, he had never before been able to come to see Her. In this year, the program was held on a Wednesday for the first time, and he was finally able to come to see Amma and to sing for Her. At the end of his song he was overcome by tears. Amma was very pleased to hear him sing with so much sincerity and devotion.

Once an old man came to stay in the ashram for a few days. Every time he went for darshan, everyone could see how sweetly Amma would embrace him. He became like a child in Her presence, even though he was quite old. Someone had given him two extra white shirts and two extra dhotis. It is traditional to offer something to the Guru, and he felt badly that he was so poor and had nothing to give Amma. He realized he did not really need both sets of clothes and decided to give one of the white shirts to Amma during his darshan. Amma was so happy to receive the shirt that She put it on immediately and wore it until the end of the darshan. Everyone went into the temple to look at Amma wearing this white shirt that blended in so well with Her sari. It was beautiful to see the old man sitting behind Her in bliss—he was overjoyed that Amma had put on his shirt. Mother just could not help Herself. She just had to wear it. From watching Amma, we could see so clearly that She finds the offering of an innocent heart irresistible.

It is very easy to be peaceful and calm when we sit with our eyes closed. However, that same attitude has to be maintained when we are actively involved in the world. When difficult situations arise for us, we need to have the same steadiness of mind that we have when the good things come to us. We should be adaptable in all circumstances, able to keep our mental equilibrium even when we are amidst stressful situations. This is the real test of how spiritually strong we have become. All we can do is try to put forth our best efforts, and then leave the rest in God's hands.

❀

> *My life has become torn in two*
> *Like a tree struck by lightening.*
> *Your love has pierced my heart*
> *And kindled a flame of desire for You.*
>
> *The cruel winds of this world*
> *Try to extinguish my love,*
> *But You protect it always*
> *And feed it with Your compassion.*
>
> *How lonely is this life,*
> *Like a sad song.*
>
> *I drift along in the midst of sorrow and delusion.*
> *Though many surround me,*
> *They belong not to me, nor I to them —*
> *You alone are embedded in my heart.*
>
> *You are like the sweet rose beyond compare*
> *In beauty and fragrance,*
> *But Your sharp thorn*
> *Is all that I can grasp.*

❀

Chapter 14

The All-Knowing Mother

*"How can Amma say who and what She is.
How can that Supreme State be explained?"*

Amma

Many years ago I came across a basket that was sitting in the passageway on the upstairs balcony at the ashram. There were about thirty packets of biscuits in this basket, and I knew it was for distribution to the brahmacharis. I felt that once it reached the brahmacharis I probably would not get any. So I thought I should probably take my share right then and there. Looking around to make sure that no one was watching me, I took one packet, put it inside my sari, and went on my way. Later on that afternoon, Amma sent one of the girls to me. The girl said, "Amma is asking if you are getting enough food to eat in the ashram?" I hesitantly choked out a "Yes," but I felt totally crushed. Amma had known what I had done, even though She had not seen it—I never was able to eat that packet of biscuits!

Amma knows everything that goes on with Her devotees. Even though She may be far away, still She knows what is happening to us and how we react in every situation.

One day a brahmachari asked Amma if She knows everything that goes on in the world, as he thought this was not possible. This fellow liked to drink tea, but in the early days it was banned from the ashram and only milk water was served. He asked Amma if She was meditating and he went to the teashop and drank tea, would She know about it? Amma said that She definitely would. Amma says that although She does not always show it, She will surely know if we do something wrong.

She may even pretend to have found out about something that we have done from another person. In this way a circumstance, either created by Amma or spontaneously occurring in Her presence, will arise that allows Her to bring all our vasanas to the surface so that they can then be removed. For instance, it may seem like Amma is looking at everyone else except us. But Amma may be just testing us to see how we react. Just as an ayurvedic doctor needs to see all of the symptoms of a patient before prescribing medicine, Amma may want to see our tendencies before knowing what sadhana to put us through.

Amma may even scold us for something that we did not do, just to see how we will respond. Although sometimes She may pretend that She knows nothing, at other times She will clearly show us that nothing escapes Her. We see only the surface of things, but Amma's vision penetrates beneath the surface and sees the past, present, and future of all situations. Our limited understanding may cause us to have doubts, but we must have faith that Amma really does know what She is doing.

Sometimes when we ask Amma a question and get an unusual answer from Her, it will seem as though She does not understand what we have said to Her. But even years later, we may suddenly understand the meaning of Her response. At other times, She may not give us answers to our questions. She has said that it is not for Her to always tell us everything, that there are some lessons we must learn from life itself.

A God-realized Soul can never make a mistake. On occasion it may seem that they are not correct—but we find in the end that they are always right. One day while we were traveling in the car someone noticed a slight burning smell. Amma insisted that something was burning in the car, but we all insisted that the burning smell was coming from the outside. As we turned into the driveway of our destination, smoke started to come from the engine. A small plastic tube was stuck near the battery and had started to melt, causing the burning smell. Once again, Amma was right. Of course, Amma is *always* right!

Amma says that She has understood the nature of Her Self, which is the same as the All-Pervading Self. Each of us is created as a miniature of the macrocosm. Therefore, if we can understand ourselves, then we can understand everything. But we have not yet learned to understand ourselves. Only a perfect Master like Amma can help us begin the process of understanding. It is said that the Master becomes our link with the Absolute Truth. Every living being possesses the seeds of enlightenment. If we discover ourselves, then we will know everything.

Amma once explained that the sun illumines everything, shining on all. There is nothing that the sun cannot touch. Yet the sun does not claim that it shines everywhere, it just humbly does its duty. In this same way, Amma in Her humility will never show that She knows everything, but through our experiences with Her, we come to understand Her true greatness.

One day in America, nearing the end of a program, someone came to me at the bookstore where I was working. She had a plate of the chocolates that Amma gives to people as prasad during darshan. As she thought of me as a responsible person, she asked if I would keep the chocolates with me for some time. Of course always being ready to help, and particularly with this type of job, I agreed to keep them with me.

As we would work for long hours during the darshan times and sometimes have lunch only in the late afternoon hours, we would often find ourselves very hungry. I guiltily opened one chocolate and popped it in my mouth. My, how delicious it was, but how to stop at one? So I opened another one or two and put them in my mouth. Suddenly the darshan program finished, and Amma started to leave the hall. In all the years that Amma had been traveling on tours, She had never once come to visit the bookstore—however, that day it seems I inspired Her to come.

I stood there in amazement as Amma walked over to me and stroked my chest. She said, "Daughter, you are looking so thin, are you eating?" All I could utter was "Mmm!" hoping I did not have a smudge of chocolate anywhere on my face. Amma replied, "The others have all put on weight, but you are looking so thin." I still could not say anything but another "Mmm," as the chocolate was dissolving in my mouth. Then Amma smiled, stroked my chest one more time, and walked off.

I felt totally embarrassed. Amma always knows exactly when to catch us off our guard and let us know that we cannot hide anything from Her. Now of course this incident happened many years ago and since then I have reformed myself. It's safe to entrust me with a plate of chocolates these days—as long as it is not before lunch!

On still another occasion Amma gave me a glimpse of Her omniscience. We were driving in the car after a program in Kuwait. Amma had let one of Her driver's young daughters ride in the car with us. This young girl who was about eight years old did not seem as close with Amma as her two sisters. She seemed shy compared with the other two. I had seen her singing for Amma that night, sitting on the back of the stage far behind where Amma was giving darshan at the front.

Amma snuggled close to her in the car. She kissed her hand and said, "You sang for Mother tonight. Amma used to sing that song a long time ago." Then Amma proceeded to sing softly the song she had sung: "*Govinda Madhava, Gopala Keshava, Jaya Nanda Mukunda Nanda Govinda, Radhe Gopala.*"

I had been watching at the time and saw that Amma never turned around to see her singing. As so many young girls had sung, I wondered how She could possibly have remembered the girl's voice as being so different from all the others? It was just another little taste of Amma's Divine motherly affection and compassionate love, shining strongly through the dark night.

Traveling with Amma, I have seen countless wishes fulfilled. Amma has the amazing ability of knowing the deepest desires of everyone's hearts. One year, during a program in Santa Fe, a devotee came up to me with a friend of his who had been born completely deaf. That day he had gone up to Amma for darshan and was astounded to *hear* Amma speaking into his ear. He could not understand how this could happen. The devotee and I smiled at each other in the understanding that this was just another one of the wonders of Amma's greatness.

Another time, a young woman from Iowa told me how her grandmother had come for darshan with terrible chronic neck pain. She told Amma of her problem. The morning after her darshan, she was amazed to find that the neck pain had completely disappeared.

A devotee in India told me that for seven years she had suffered from terrible migraines and could not eat rice or any fruit. When She went for darshan, Amma fed her some rice. Since then, her headaches and food allergies have completely disappeared and she is able to eat normally again. She feels that with Amma's grace she has been healed.

Amma once visited a devotee who was in the hospital being treated for burns. When Amma saw him there, She kissed both his hands and his feet, and gave him some prasad. Later he cried while telling this story to another devotee, explaining that it was his birthday, and he had always had a strong desire for Amma to kiss his hands. He was deeply moved that She had fulfilled his desire.

Although Amma has millions of devotees around the globe, She has a relationship with each and every one of them. When we were in Munich one year, Amma asked about an old woman who in the past had come to see Her every year. She had not seen this lady, and so was asking all of us if we remembered her or knew where she was. I could not remember the old woman, and none of the others could remember her either. But Amma was emphatic that we should find out about this woman, as Amma said Her mind kept dwelling on her.

This old woman used to tell Amma that she was all alone in the world, that there was no one else for her except for Amma. Every year she would look forward to coming to see Her. Amma kept asking each one of us about her, but no one could give Her any information about the old woman. She said it was our *dharma* to find out about her. Eventually, we discovered that this woman had died one month before Amma's visit. Even though none of us could remember her, her memory had been firmly imprinted in Amma's heart.

When we travel to different states in India and around the world, Amma's satsang is always translated into the local language. It is quite amazing to watch Amma enact the drama of listening to and correcting the satsang even though it is in another language. Amma never fails to catch any mistake the translator may make, even though She does not know the language. Someone once asked Amma if She understands all the different languages or if She could simply read peoples' thoughts? Amma answered that even if She does not know the language, Her mind will tell Her if someone is making a mistake.

Amma has true knowledge about everything, even though She attended school only until the fourth grade. For example, She holds conversations with nuclear scientists, advising them about different aspects of their work. These men may have dedicated their entire lives to the study of complicated subjects like nuclear physics, mathematics, relativity, and quantum mechanics; but still Amma points out different facts that they had never quite grasped or understood throughout their numerous years of study and work in the field. Though Her formal education may have only lasted a few years, Her knowledge arises quite clearly and spontaneously.

What Amma is able to orchestrate at any one moment is quite miraculous. For example, just imagine the scene at a Sunday Devi Bhava in India. There are usually a minimum of 10,000 to 15,000 people who come for darshan. At the beginning of the darshan, it is my job to hand the prasad to Amma, so I usually sit near Her. The speakers blast out the bhajans so loudly that they vibrate, and one has to shout to be heard above the music. I often have to battle just to try to get a piece of prasad into Amma's hand on time for Her to give it to each person. I struggle trying to do only one thing, while Amma effortlessly does ten other things at once.

Can you imagine a line of twenty hungry babies all waiting to be thrust into Amma's lap for Her to feed them their first solid food of sweetened rice? Small babies, but with huge lung capacities, screaming and crying all at the same time, flailing their tiny arms around and squirming in Amma's lap. Amma tries to stick the rice in their mouths, and at the same time the administrators from AIMS sit on Her left side asking questions about the hospital. The brahmacharis who run the computer institutes and engineering schools wait to put their questions in too. At the same time, a boy hangs over Amma's right shoulder trying to get Her attention. *"Amme! Amme!* (poking at Her), *Amme! Amme!* I have got this slight pain in my left elbow. Look, Amma, look. Can you touch it for me, Amma? Amma, touch it! Amma, touch it!"

Then every third person that comes for darshan says, "Mantra, Amma, I want a mantra." Amma gives mantras on the right side, whispering in peoples' ears. She answers questions one by one, while still looking over at the girls to console someone who is crying and saying, "Amma never looks at me, I don't think She loves me anymore."

The darshan still goes on, thousands of people per hour. A westerner asks, "Name, Amma, I want a name." Meanwhile the boy hanging over Her right shoulder says, *"Amme! Amme!* Can I bring you something to drink, Amma? Can I bring you something to drink, Amma? Amma, the pain has gotten a bit less, but perhaps you should touch my arm again just so it doesn't come back. And maybe you can touch the other arm too, just in case." Amma has to stroke both his arms before he will leave Her alone.

Amma does everything at once with Her full concentration. I try to do just one thing and find that difficult.

One time at the end of a Devi Bhava, I needed to ask Amma an important question for somebody. She had given darshan to 15,000 people non-stop and had stayed up all night without any sleep. When Devi Bhava finally ended, it was mid-morning of the next day. I was exhausted due to lack of sleep, but Amma was still going strong. I went to Her room and asked the question. Amma gave the answer, and then proceeded to chat about other subjects. She ended up telling me the whole history of India from ancient times to present day. She was the perfect history teacher. It took about thirty minutes.

During the conversation, She even worked out mathematical equations in Her head. She said, "Now if 680,000 is divided by 28, we get 24,285, and if this is multiplied by 18 that makes 437,141. No, no, 437,142. That's right, isn't it?" Well, my head was absolutely spinning just trying to follow Her. There was no way I would have attempted to add those figures without a calculator, but Amma's mind is brilliant.

On another occasion, Amma wanted some figures worked out while we were traveling on an airplane. I did not have a calculator with me, so I ended up writing everything on paper, and then adding up this long list of numbers. This process took me about ten minutes, and at the end I showed it to Amma. She looked at it for a few seconds and said, "I think you made one small mistake in addition, right here." She zoomed right in on that mistake out of a whole page of figures.

One night when we were on tour in Santa Fe, I was staying in the room next to Amma. While I often stayed near Amma's room, in the last few years I had not had the opportunity to sleep in the room with Her as I had occasionally done in the early years. Suddenly, it crossed my mind how nice it would be to lie down near Amma and to hold Her. The thought surprised me, as I was usually happy to be in the background and was not often yearning as most people do to be so physically close to Amma. But the thought quickly passed through my mind and was gone, and I went to sleep.

A few hours later, during the night, somebody came and told me that Amma was calling for me. I went into the room and Amma asked me to massage Her legs. Because of the altitude and climate in New Mexico, Amma would often go for several nights without sleeping, as She had done on this occasion. So I massaged Her legs, hoping this would help Her to rest. After a while She said to me, "Only if you lie down next to Amma and hold Her, might Mother be able to sleep." This totally surprised me, but I did, and Amma went quickly to sleep.

Even just a fleeting desire of mine, Amma had fulfilled so quickly. What to say of the heartfelt prayers of ours that She is so much more likely to fulfill?

Can't You hear the cry of my anguished heart?
Don't You see my burning tears fall?
The world has lost its sweetness.
I long only to drink
The nectar of Your compassionate form.
My heart is torn by this unrequited love.

I wait here with a trembling heart
Knowing I am not worthy to offer myself to You.
What can this wretched soul do?
I am drowning in a sea of sorrow.

Chapter 15

Transforming Lives

*"Even the smallest thing that we do for the sake of others
can bring about a great transformation in society.
We may not get to see the change at once,
but every good action certainly has its rewards.
Even a smile is extremely valuable,
and a smile costs us nothing!"*

Amma

There was once a man who wanted to change the world. He prayed, "O Lord, give me the energy to change this world." Later, when many years passed by and he became middle aged, he realized he did not have enough strength to change the world. He was no longer young and rebellious. So he began to pray, "O Lord, give me enough energy to change my relatives." They were much younger and stronger and not interested in changing. So then he began to pray, "Give me enough strength to change myself." Only then was he satisfied. If we change ourselves, then all else follows.

All great spiritual Masters say that happiness is not found in the outside world, but lies within us. A Mahatma does not come to change the world, but to inspire us to create change within ourselves. They will not do all the work for us, but will be the catalyst and inspiration for us to transform.

We can try to alter every external thing in our lives in order to be more spiritual. We can change our name, move to a foreign country, eat different food, or get a nose ring just like Amma's. We can change these external things, but if our minds remain the same, all our problems will follow us wherever we go. Our fears and anxieties will always stay the same. External situations can be changed, but only a great Master like Amma can remove fears and anxieties from our lives by changing our hearts. Amma transforms us from the inside by helping us realize the truth of our Divine Nature.

One devotee told me that since meeting Amma, she has stopped buying new saris. All the money she used to spend on buying new saris, she now saves up and gives to Amma to be used for the poor, because Amma has inspired her to live more simply.

A woman from Mysore shared that after learning Amma's *IAM* meditation, her life vastly improved. A widowed mother of three, this woman worked in Amma's school as a sweeper, putting in twelve hours of hard work each day. She said that before learning the technique, she suffered from an aching body, asthma and fatigue. Since practicing IAM regularly, all of these symptoms have disappeared. She said that she is still aware of problems that exist in her life, but she does not pay attention to them and does not worry so much anymore. She now surrenders her problems to Amma. Her life has become peaceful.

Most people in the world are so unhappy. Young people grow up not knowing what to turn to in their lives to give them peace or satisfaction. But children who grow up knowing Amma learn to cultivate good qualities right from the beginning. Such was the case with a young French boy that came on tour in India with his mother. At seven years old, he usually read his books or amused himself in some way. During one of the programs in Mysore, I was surprised to see him out in the crowd serving water to the devotees. He was carrying a glass and a jug of water, moving down the aisles happily offering water to the thirsty devotees, like the other grown-up volunteers that had been assigned to do this seva. By the influence of being around Amma and Her devotees, the desire to serve others was forming in his young mind.

A lot of people come to Amma never having understood what life is about or why they exist. Through their contact with Amma, their values and desires in life have been remolded, giving them a meaningful and happy existence.

While we were in Munich, holding a program at a venue that was situated near a famous beer drinking area, a drunken man stumbled into the program off the street where he just happened to be walking past. He could not quite work out what was going on, but when Amma gave him darshan on Her way out at the end of the program, She was utterly charming with him. The next evening he turned up again, groomed and sober, keen to experience another dose of Amma's Divine Love, a much stronger brew than he had ever tasted before. Today he does not miss any of Amma's programs in Germany, and he sometimes comes to India for a few months to stay in the ashram.

For some people the journey to visit Amma in India is hard; the climate and heat, the food and the crowds are a burden for their bodies to bear. The unfamiliar language, customs and traditions are difficult for them to understand. But they are willing to undergo any kind of hardship for another taste of Amma's unconditional love.

An Italian man in his eighties used to come on the North Indian tours for many years, as he said that he found them very invigorating. Even with the grueling bus trips and long program hours, he said that he acquired more energy from the tours. Some younger people found it much more tiring than he did, but he was so surrendered to the situations he encountered on the tour that he was able to find joy and enthusiasm in almost any circumstance.

Some people may misunderstand the meaning of surrender in leading a spiritual life. They may think that it implies weakness, by blindly obeying commands or rules. But no one is trying to make slaves out of us. In fact, we are already slaves to our own attachments, which cause us great sorrow. If we can learn how to surrender our attachments, Amma will guide us every step of the way to freedom. For many, the first step is learning the art of letting go, the art of releasing our egoistic grip on life and gradually letting go of our attachments and expectations. In order to eradicate the selfishness that binds and enslaves us, we must strive to develop the qualities of love and compassion that Amma embodies. Amma is trying to show us how to make ourselves free, truly free. This is very difficult for us to do on our own, but with Amma's grace anything is possible.

When we ordinary humans look at each other, we tend to see only the ugliness of the other's ego. But great Saints such as Amma look at us and see only the divinity that lies within us. They see the purity and magnificence of our souls, the perfection and divine potential that lies untapped in us. We may look at each other and see only pieces of rock, but Amma sees us as

tiny diamonds. Just as diamonds need polishing to smooth off the rough edges, we also need to undergo a polishing process.

It is Amma's duty to finish off this process. She says She really does not have to do anything to us at all. She just puts everyone together, and the process happens automatically. It seems we all have our little ways of rubbing against each other and creating friction, and this is all that is necessary to polish off our rough edges. All She has to do is press the button to start the process. And Amma really knows how to press our buttons!

Often we may not be able to see change within ourselves, but others may notice the differences in us. When we walk along the beach, we may be looking down and not realize how far we have come until we reach the end. Then, when we look back, it is hard to believe the distance we have traveled. Similarly, we should strive to change, even if we cannot immediately see what we have gained from our previous efforts.

There are some people who meet Amma and immediately their lives are transformed. Other devotees over the years slowly think of renouncing the things that they are attached to in the world. Some return home after visiting Amma's ashram in India and realize that things that were fulfilling them do not anymore. Maybe they stop going to movies or drinking alcohol. They keep better company and spend more time with other devotees who attend satsang.

For many, it is initially Amma's darshan that deeply moves them and initiates a process of change. One woman described that over the years she has noticed she has become more comfortable with herself and relates to people more easily. Slowly, she has become more service-minded, realizing that next to Amma's darshan, the closest she can feel to God is in doing selfless service. Though the changes have been slow, she feels that there is nowhere to go but towards a more spiritual life.

This slow process of spiritual unfolding is more long-lasting than sudden change. When people move forward too quickly, they tend to go back to their old ways because the vasanas are too deep and hard to get rid of all at once. A jackal may claim that it will no longer howl at the moon and will succeed in holding to its word for a full month—until the full moon comes out again!

Thousands of people have come to Amma, experienced Her Divine Love, and developed a whole new outlook on life. Their lives really have been transformed. In the village where Amma grew up, numerous villagers were opposed to the ashram during the early years, but today are strong supporters. Even Amma's brothers-in-law were initially against the ashram. However, in marrying Amma's sisters, they have grown into some of Amma's most fervent devotees.

A lady from Switzerland had a moving experience to share about meeting Amma. She had suffered a deep mental depression and had eventually entered a psychiatric hospital. The following year she met Amma and took a long list of questions to ask Her, hoping that She would take away her illness. Amma answered only that she should meditate ten minutes each day. The woman felt she did not have the strength to do so. She was able to leave the hospital three months later, but without much hope of overcoming her illness.

Even though it was clear to her that Amma was a Mahatma, she felt that even Amma was not able to help her overcome her terrible depression. She felt doomed by her illness, like she was in a prison with no way out. Her sister once asked Amma what else she could do to help her. Amma replied, "Tell your sister that she is under Amma's protection."

Even with her illness, she joined her ninety-year-old mother in laminating photos and stickers that were being made for sale in the bookstore. Gradually, she began to feel some contentment that she could help others through this selfless service.

The next year, when Amma visited their town for the tour, this lady joined Her for a walk around the grounds of her sister's house where Amma was staying. During the walk, Amma sat down on a small wooden footbridge to meditate, and this lady sat with the others by the side of the river. Listening to the bubbling noise of the water, she suddenly felt that the heavy weight on her shoulders was flowing away with the water. The next night she had another powerful revelation when Amma came back from the program hall early in the morning. Amma passed her on the stairs and touched her hand. Through Amma's physical touch, she experienced in a split second that *Amma is the Real Truth*. She felt deep within that she was accepted by God and not condemned as she had always thought.

This lady feels that Mother had worked on her from within. Perhaps it was the acts of service that brought the grace to create a healing. With Amma's grace, She was able to stop taking antidepressants, and feels convinced that Amma's IAM meditation helps her to keep her inner balance. She has been relieved of the serious depression that filled so many years of her life with darkness. It is as if she has had a second chance in life.

When we come into Amma's presence and start yearning to become one with Her, all that is within us that is not in harmony with Her Divine Love and perfect purity just naturally starts to come up. Then it can be either eradicated or transformed for the better. Only when we become aware of our weaknesses can we begin to consciously work on transforming them.

Amma has given everyone a new beginning. With the fresh understanding of what the goal of life is really supposed to be, Amma has initiated, through the power of Her love, the prospect of living a meaningful life wherever we may be in the world. She offers Her own life as the perfect example of good qualities for us to strive to imbibe and emulate. Amma is inspiring many millions around the world to help, love, and serve humanity.

The changes occurring in people are like the caterpillar who spins its cocoon—it remains encased inside for some time, then breaks out of its shell in the form of a colorful butterfly spreading its beauty and wonder around the world. Amma metamorphoses Her children into such wonderful butterflies. The cocoon of Amma's love that is wrapped around each one of us nurtures us and creates a magical transformation. We are then set free in the world to enhance the beauty of Her creation.

Can you imagine the delight on Amma's face as She watches Her butterflies flutter around Her, Her white sari gently blowing in the breeze? With a smile and a laugh, She basks in the joy of creating such beautiful butterflies to chase away the sorrows of the world and to add another exquisite touch to Her creation.

How I long to behold Your beauteous form,
but with even a glimpse of You
My impure eyes must fall.
Your lotus eyes
filled with love and compassion,
melt my wicked heart.
My dream of You
is all I can hold onto,
So close,
but yet so far away.

Chapter 16

❦

Rebuilding Bodies, Minds and Souls

"There is always a divine message hidden
in the seemingly negative experiences we go through.
We just have to penetrate beneath the surface of a situation
and the message will be revealed.
But we usually remain on the outer surface."

Amma

They called it Black Sunday, the day after Christmas, December 2004, when the tsunami hit South-east Asia and India. Lives were changed. They will never be the same again. One can rebuild broken homes, but how to rebuild broken lives? When one has helplessly seen life extinguished right in front of their eyes, how can one ever remain the same?

Thousands of people in coastal villages lost their lives. Countless more lost their homes, in fact, lost everything in the swiftly moving tidal waves that rocked the shores. Most people living near the ashram had little to start off with; now they had nothing. Many parents in the villages lost their children. Although they tried their best to hold them in their arms when the sea came rushing in, the flood of water was too strong, and their children were swept away. How to face the world again when you have seen your own children swept from your arms?

We heard stories of people who watched helplessly, as one or more of their family members drowned. One man was holding on to his father but lost his grip, and he had to watch his father go under, right in front of his eyes. He will never be the same again. Some women complain that they are unable to sleep at night, for when they lie down to rest, the scene of the flood replays in their head and brings with it such a painful headache. There are so many heartbreaking tales of loss, and the whole community has grieved for the widespread suffering, not just here in India but in other countries as well.

Amma had forewarned during the summer tour of 2003, that there might be great catastrophes worldwide in 2005. But She said there was nothing we could do except pray. The ashram astrologer had remarked to me just the day before that December 26th would be the beginning of a bad period. Neither of us had any idea what an understatement this would be. Even during the morning program on the day of the tsunami, Amma had an ominous feeling that something bad was going to happen. She was frantically trying to finish the darshan quickly. A brahmachari had reported a strange phenomenon to Her, that the ocean waters had receded. Amma knew that what went out had to come back, and so She advised that all the vehicles should be moved from the seashore side around to the mainland. There were numerous ashram vehicles, buses, and devotees' cars, around 200, but these were all saved because of Amma's forethought. Amma had also instructed that everything that was on the ground floor of the Ayurveda building, which is right by the seashore, should be moved to higher floors.

As soon as Amma was informed of the rising waters just outside the walls of the ashram, She began to give instructions for how to deal with the potential hazard. She told that the electricity should be turned off, and that the nearby town should be informed to turn off the transformer that supplied electricity to the whole island, saving us from any cases of electrocution. Before long, a torrential flow of water swept through the ashram, rising at least waist-high and much higher in some places. When the waters began to subside, Amma waded through the murky overflow. She surveyed the situation and started overseeing the evacuation of visitors, residents, and local people that had sought refuge in the ashram.

The AICT (Amrita Institute of Computer Technology) and Amrita Engineering School across the backwaters became shelters for thousands of people, many of whom had lost their homes. The newly constructed Ayurveda School became an emergency site for those villagers missing a family member and a hospital for the sick or injured. In addition, all of Amma's schools functioned as emergency shelters. Amma saw that food was provided for the several thousands of people affected, and a clothing distribution was organized for the villagers who had lost everything. Amma visited the local devotees consoling and comforting them in this time of irreparable loss.

After the flood, Amma assured the safety and protection of Her children every step of the way, including Her animal children. When everyone was evacuated from the ashram, Amma firmly declared that She would not leave until the elephants and cows had been taken first. In fear of the waters rising again, She made sure the animals were safely secured in the temple building, which was starting to look a little like Noah's Ark! Later that evening, after midnight, when the cows had been safely

brought into the temple and the elephants had been walked an hour and a half from the ashram down the peninsula and around the mainland, only then did Amma leave.

When Amma reached the other side of the backwaters we noticed that Her lips were dry. She had refused to take even a sip of water the whole day. How could She drink when so many had died? For days following the devastation Amma walked barefoot. From the time She left the ashram and crossed the backwaters and even as She made visits around the grounds and to the refugee camps set up at the institutes, She refused to wear Her sandals. It was as if She had taken a resolve not to wear shoes while so many people were suffering.

Until early morning on the night of the flood, Amma tirelessly told the story of the tsunami again and again to all the devotees who were calling the ashram, worried about everyone there. One *brahmacharini,* who lives in a branch school away from the ashram in another state, said that only after hearing Amma tell the details of the day and all of the events that had occurred was her mind able to rest. Amma knew this, which is why She made the effort to give everyone who worried about us, some peace of mind. Even over the phone, Amma tried to console others and bring them solace.

Devotees demonstrated that they had absorbed Amma's teachings on non-attachment and renunciation during the emergency evacuation. At the time of evacuation, most of the visitors and residents had nothing with them but the one set of clothes they had been wearing that day. No mat to lie on, no shawl to cover with at night, not even a toothbrush. But people found they were happily making do, without being surrounded by their normal personal belongings. Sadly remembering those who had lost everything made it easier to be thankful for the clothes on their backs and a safe, dry place to sleep.

People all over the world opened up their hearts in response to the suffering that befell so many. Amma's body, mind and soul cried out for these people. She was able to offer not only monetary and physical relief, but also the consolation of their hearts and souls. Amma asked everyone to join in offering prayers for the living as well as those who had been taken away from this earth in that moment of tragedy.

A lady from Chennai recounted a story for us. She said that she had seen on television a poor woman and her son who were hungry, and waiting for their food delivery. When the truck delivering their meal finally arrived, they were handed out food packets. By the look on the woman's face, there was a foul smell coming from the packet. Although they were extremely hungry, she was unable to eat when she smelled the spoiled food. So she and her son reluctantly put the food packet under a tree. A dog came by and sniffed this food packet—even the dog refused to eat it. This spoilage of food often happens when hot food is packaged before cooling.

Relief agencies were trying to help, but unfortunately they were not under the supervision of someone like Amma, who lovingly made sure that the food served to people was not in packets, but served fresh and hot in large vessels brought straight from the kitchens. She knew how sad the people were, so She went to extraordinary lengths to make sure that the particular rice and food that they liked was cooked.

Only Amma really knows the hearts of those in sorrow. While we may often think of words of consolation to offer to people, this may not have a profound effect on them. But just one caring touch from Amma, with maybe not even any words spoken or a silent tear shed while just holding them close, is enough to dispel some of their sorrows.

Mother was so distraught about the situation of the people who had nothing that She spent hours one night stitching petticoats for the village ladies. She has since donated sewing machines and offered training for women to learn tailoring so that they can have some form of livelihood for the future.

Even though the ashram did not sustain any structural damage, putrid water and mud flowed through all the ground floor offices and storage rooms. Everyone worked together with great love, enthusiasm and devotion to salvage what we could from the wreckage. We cleaned every single area, working hard, but happy to do so in such a time of need.

All of the ashram residents and visitors also helped in the relief efforts for the villagers. One older man from Germany who was constantly working in the kitchen said, "My only prayer is to let me be able to do something useful for others. I am only sad that I am an old man now and could have done much more to help if I were younger." Indian devotees sent truckloads of clothes to be donated to the villagers whose homes had been destroyed. For days, women worked together to sort and fold the mountains of clothing.

Within four days of deciding to relocate the refugees from the tsunami, the ashram's temporary accommodation was almost completely finished. Residents and other helpers worked night and day to try to finish these shelters for the people that needed them. The brahmachari in charge of the construction of the shelters worked tirelessly. Amma phoned him every two hours throughout the night to check on the progress. He was always there, foregoing sleep for days to try to finish these buildings that were so badly needed. Nine shelters were completed within five days by the ashram.

It is difficult to describe the love with which Amma's devotees work. The attitude with which they perform their actions is something that only another devotee can really understand. People who seek only material pleasures will never know the type of love with which these volunteers perform their work.

For months after the tsunami, Amma continued to feed almost 27,000 people three meals a day, both in Kerala and Tamil Nadu. She insisted that the refugees should eat first, and the ashram residents should eat only afterwards, in the true spirit of putting others before ourselves.

Although the coastal villages of Kerala will never ever be the same, they have the grace for Amma to be near them, watching over them and helping when She can. When one reporter asked Amma how She could commit to 23 million dollars for tsunami relief in South India, Amma replied, "The ashram residents work day in and day out, and they don't take any payment for their work. They do all the driving and the construction and operate the earthmovers. There are no contractors. All the materials—bricks, windows, doors, and furniture—are made by our brahmacharis. We do all the electrical, plumbing and structural work. This building work is nothing new for us. For years we have been providing free houses for the destitute in forty-seven sites throughout India."

Amma went on to say that it was all because of the selfless work of the devotees that Amma has been able to accomplish so many things. Amma does not proclaim to do anything Herself. She never has. Right from the beginning, with the very first miracle that She performed, She claims it was done with the hands of other people. That is how humble She is.

After the flood, some Gujarati men came down to help in the relief work. They had collected rice and numerous items for the villagers, but sadly found that to hire a truck to transport it all to Kerala would cost much more than the items were worth. So they donated all the goods to the local government in Amma's name, and decided to travel to the ashram to help. They told Amma, "You were there for us when we needed help, and now that Amma's village has been destroyed, we want to help you to rebuild." Amma was extremely touched by their sincere gesture, so She sent them off to the construction site to help with the work of building temporary shelters.

At the time of the tsunami, over 15,000 people were gathered together at the ashram, right on the coast; but by Amma's grace, not even one person was injured. Although so many hundreds of thousands of people perished from the tsunami, many people survived and their stories reveal that grace alone saved them.

One British school child was on vacation with her family in Thailand and saved hundreds of people. She had just studied about tsunamis at school and knew from watching the ocean withdraw that they had about ten minutes before a powerful wave would hit the coastal village. She informed her mother of this and the entire area was evacuated. Countless lives were saved because of one small child.

A five-year-old Indonesian boy was playing in his home when the tsunami hit and swept him far out into the ocean. He survived for two days at sea floating on a mattress. He said that he was not afraid, as he was used to playing in the water, although he had been extremely cold. Eventually some fishermen rescued him, but it was grace alone that truly saved him.

A man from one of the Nicobar Islands was pulled under by the powerful waters. When he was thrown back to the land he realized he was the only person from the island who had survived. He lived on coconuts for twenty-five days until the army rescued him. People from other islands also survived for more than forty-five days like this.

Nothing happens accidentally. When natural disasters occur, or in incidents such as when the towers of the World Trade Centers collapsed, it is destiny for people to be drawn to that spot at that time when it is their karma to leave the body. The body may perish, but the Atman remains ever indestructible.

A reporter asked Amma if the tsunami was a message from Mother Nature. She replied that nature is telling us that she should not be exploited. But even so soon after a tragedy, already everyone is pretending to be asleep, which shows that we have not learned from this lesson. That is why perhaps more bad things will happen, because we are not learning the lesson that Mother Nature is trying to teach us.

Amma says, "Whatever we are experiencing now is a result of our past actions. By doing right actions in the present we can pave the way for a better tomorrow. There is no point brooding about the past. Instead, we can try to share the grief of those left behind. We must light the lamp of love in our hearts and extend our helping hands to all those suffering around us."

This small fish once used to swim in the sea of delusion.
The waves of sorrow raged on endlessly
Through the deep dark waters,
But You offered a shelter
In the midst of the stormy seas —
A cave where You dwelt
Where misery could not enter,
A refuge for us lonely lost souls.
I gladly sought Your shelter
And You took me in with Your loving compassion.
I no longer seek to swim in that sea of delusion
As I know the calm, sweet refuge
With You always lies waiting.

Chapter 17

Tapping Our Inner Strength

"Love and beauty are within you.
Try to express them through your actions
and you will definitely touch the very source of bliss."

Amma

About fifteen years ago an incident occurred that clearly stuck in my memory. We were a few people sitting in a room with Amma. She turned to me and started to sing a few lines from a song. Some of the brahmacharis that were in the room turned to see who Amma was singing to. As half of them smiled and half of them looked sad, I was very curious to know what the words of the song meant, so I asked someone.

Roughly translated, the words of the song had been, "Because you were born as a woman, it is your destiny to cry." I have always remembered this. It has been the destiny of women all through history, even from the very beginning of creation, to suffer—either at the hands of others or because of the state of their own minds. Amma knows well the pain and anguish women have had to bear. She has decided that there has been enough suffering for women from time immemorial. In order to overcome this suffering, we must find the strength inherent in our spiritual selves, which will allow us to fully embody our inner divine nature.

Over the years, Amma has been invited to speak at several conferences. It is not Her way to push teachings on anyone—She says that the knowledge must be drawn out from Her. And so, as fate would have it, Amma was invited to speak at the Global Peace Initiative of Women Religious and Spiritual Leaders at the United Nations in Geneva, Switzerland. Her speech, *The Awakening of Universal Motherhood*, was based on Her experience of growing up in an oppressive society. In Her speech, Amma encouraged women to cultivate their inner qualities of compassion, patience and understanding, and to re-awaken these traits that lie dormant in every woman. Amma called on women to rise up and take action against the suffering that had been handed down to them for so many years.

Amma grew up in an environment that had many harsh and strict rules for girls, but She did not allow these oppressive customs to affect Her. Amma's mother used to tell Her that the earth should not even feel the step of a woman, and that the walls should not hear her speak. When Her family had guests in the house, the girls would have to remain in their rooms as they were not to be seen or heard by the visitors. Although She was taller than Her younger brother, Amma would have to stand when he entered a room.

Despite this stifling upbringing, Amma's inner strength was never diminished. In fact, the difficulties made Her stronger and helped Her develop deeper compassion and a greater understanding for how most women in the world live. In spite of punishment from Her family, Amma held firmly to Her commitment to try to help others in need. In time, Her family realized that Amma's inner strength could not be compromised;

it was a shining light that refused to be dimmed, and would shed its light to relieve the suffering of those around Her.

When Amma spoke about Motherhood in Geneva, She was not delivering a speech about a theoretical concept. She expresses this quality every minute of Her life. Even as a child She mothered Her family and neighbors. People meeting Her for the first time repeatedly tell us how they cannot explain the soul-stirring effect She has on them, and many simply burst into tears. Such is the power of Amma's Divine Love. Amma, with only a fourth grade education, has achieved the unimaginable simply by remaining centered in the "Power of Motherhood."

A man in America once wanted to argue against some of Amma's statements in Her speech. He said that Amma came from only a small village, and up in North India where he had come from, it is actually the women that are the heads of the households.

Amma turned to him and emphatically declared, "Do you think that Amma is a small frog in a small well? She is like a big frog in the ocean!" Amma continued to tell this man that She speaks from Her experience of seeing over thirty million people during the last thirty years; and over half of them being women, of wiping away the tears of their sorrows and trying to comfort them.

It is indeed a miracle how Amma is changing countless lives through the power of Motherhood. She is showing the whole world that it is working, and that if men and women work together, they will not only restore harmony to society, but will also reclaim their real identity as true human beings. When we realize our true potential, we will find ourselves capable of so much more than we would have thought. Amma's inexhaustible

love for us inspires us to have the strength to reach beyond our limitations and start to live our lives in a more selfless manner.

Amma knows the capabilities that we have. She wants women to be able to do everything for themselves. On the practical level, Amma wants us to become strong and self-sufficient in all areas. In the ashram, She asked women to take over doing things that men used to do, like purchasing and accounting. In Amma's institutions in India, women are the heads of departments and the principals of schools. On a North India Tour one year, Amma wanted all the women to load the bags and equipment on top of the buses, something that the men usually do.

After the tsunami, Amma sent many of the brahmacharinis out to help clean the village houses. These girls spent long days shoveling sand and moving rubble and debris, all out of their love for Amma. For days straight they worked in the heat to relieve others' suffering.

Amma put two girls in charge of the night security work at the site where the new houses were being constructed at a little distance from the ashram. We were all surprised at this, thinking it was work that was not so suitable for females. Yet Amma insisted that Her girls have so much courage, so why should they not do this work?

Once, during a Devi Bhava, I saw a brahmacharini tell her problem to Amma. In answer to her problem, Amma made this girl show her biceps and said, "See! You've got muscles; you can do it!"

Women sometimes complain that it seems they have to work so much harder than men. One time I asked Amma about how a woman loses her spiritual energy, as a man may lose his energy through the loss of semen. Amma replied that a woman loses her spiritual energy through her thoughts and emotions. This is why women usually end up having to do more physical work than men, so they can channel their thoughts and emotions in a positive direction rather than losing their mental and emotional strength.

Never before has a being as great as Amma been known to the world. No one but Amma has touched so many and shown such extraordinary love and concern with Her physical body. Amma has infinite patience and compassion. She gives the love of a mother, and this is what the world needs. The power of that love may be slow acting, but it is greater and more potent than anything else in the world. We do not have to give birth to understand motherhood, for Amma tells us that its essence is love; it is an attitude in the mind.

People often ask how Amma can go on sitting for hours on end and give darshan with so little sleep or food. Amma has a human body but She is not conscious of Her body. When She sees crowds of people out there suffering so much, She says She just has to go on. She has to see everyone to the last person. Amma is capable of so much because by the sheer power of Her mind She can overcome all bodily limitations. She is an example to us all, and calls on us to tap into our own inner strength, to go beyond our perceived limitations.

Amma's tour schedules are extremely rigorous. For any one of us to keep up with Her, we must call forth some inner strength. No normal person can uphold such a challenging and demanding schedule on their own. Instead, we let Amma work through us. In this surrender, we find we are able to go beyond what we thought we would be able to do. For most of us, sometimes we feel we are being pushed to the limit, but then we find we can always go a little further. Often people cannot understand why or how we can do so much, but we find we get the strength to be able to do what we have to do when it is an action with love behind it. As with a mother carrying a child for nine months, the weight of the child may seem unendurable at times, yet the mother surrenders to bearing it because of her love.

On the North India Tour last year when we were in Bhopal, we were traveling to the evening program, and Amma was not feeling well. In fact, She was extremely sick. I had medication for Her, but She refused to take it. Knowing how She had been feeling, we worried how She would make it through the darshan with 100,000 people waiting for Her. Yet She still went on, giving darshan throughout the whole night and next morning. Amma again and again inspires us to rise above and go beyond what we think our limitations are.

There is a famous story about the Titanic. As the ship began to sink, people rushed to climb into lifeboats. One lifeboat had too many people on board. Someone announced that the boat was too full. If at least one person would volunteer to go overboard, then they would all be saved. One man very courageously dived overboard and gave his life to all the others. This brave young man tapped into his inner strength to be able to sacrifice his life for others. When we realize that Amma is sacrificing Herself everyday for suffering humanity, we cannot help but want to offer our lives in service as well.

During the Amritavarsham50 celebrations, Amma made a visit to AIMS to attend the CEO Summit being held there. In the front entrance of the conference room, there was an elaborate flower design on the floor. Amma is usually very careful about not disturbing these designs, but on this day She was looking up at all the people and did not notice the flower mandala. She inadvertently walked into the corner of it, and then proceeded to walk straight towards the stage.

After being seated on the stage, Amma reached down and pulled a big thick pin from the sole of Her foot. She handed the pin to me. I was shocked, and felt terribly sick at the thought of the pain that must have been in Amma's foot, knowing how much it can hurt if we get just a small pin prick, let alone a one-inch long, thick pin lodged directly into our foot. Although I was completely disturbed thinking of Amma's pain, Amma did not even bat an eyelid. She continued listening to the speeches by the invited guests and then gave Her own satsang.

I quietly tried to arrange for Amma's shoes to be brought and for an alcohol swab and a band-aid so I could surreptitiously treat the wound to prevent infection. Although I asked two different people to arrange for these things, nothing was forthcoming.

After the program, which lasted an hour, Amma went into a smaller room to meet with some of the CEO's. I finally acquired an alcohol swab and a band-aid for Amma, and I was able to quickly swab Her foot. When I tried to put the band-aid on, Amma took it from my hand, as She had started to receive the guest speakers for darshan. Twice I tried to take the band-aid from Her, so She would have Her hands free, but She would not let me take it. Amma then called another thirty people for darshan, while She continued to hold the band-aid in the palm of Her hand. After the darshan, She walked through the hospital and stopped to visit a dying patient for some time. As we passed through the hospital wards, Amma stopped to caress a few babies in the pediatric intensive care unit. All of this time She walked without Her shoes.

When we finally got into the car to return to the birthday site, Amma opened Her hand and I saw that She was still holding the band-aid and had been for the last hour. Amma refused to let anyone look at Her foot for She was never thinking of Her own comfort; She was too busy thinking of the needs of hundreds of thousands of devotees.

The next day Amma realized that Her foot was starting to get infected and decided to take antibiotics. She took them on an empty stomach, which made Her feel ill; but She kept giving darshan for over nineteen hours, embracing nearly 50,000 people. Amma told me later that at one time during the darshan She could not even see. She said that Her vision had totally diminished and the crowd simply "swam" in front of Her eyes. No one knew this, as She still went on embracing people for hours.

I later mentioned to the girls who made the flower design that they should never use pins, as it is dangerous. They answered that they had not used any pins. I personally felt that with this incident Amma was absorbing any kind of negativity that was due to happen at the time of the birthday, as the four-day event involving so many people miraculously took place without a single accident or injury.

A journalist once asked Amma what the secret of Her success is. Amma suggested that maybe it is that people are finding in Her what is essential for all, but what is missing in them. When prompted further, Amma said, "It is Love." Amma added, "There are two types of poverty: material poverty and poverty of love and compassion. If love and compassion are awakened, then the other kind of poverty is also done away with."

Amma's compassion and love give Her the strength to accomplish incredible things and to influence millions of lives around the world. Compassion is the expression of love and has the capacity to remove suffering. It blossoms as the fruit of true understanding and provides us with the strength to do anything.

I yearn to sing You a long sad song,
to bring tears to Your eyes and to melt Your heart.
Just to make You shed one tear for me,
as I have shed oceans for You.
But as memory of You comes to my mind,
all words fade away.
You who transcend all gunas -
then how to speak of Thee?

No words can hold Your glory,
no tune can convey Your beauty.
You have stolen the beauty and glory from all things
and contain it within Yourself.
And also You have stolen my heart.
Only my tears fall and You are left unmoved.

Chapter 18

✿

Finding Heaven on Earth

*"Contentment and happiness depend solely on the mind,
not on external objects or circumstances.
Both heaven and hell are created by the mind."*

Amma

People often think that God exists only up in the sky, sitting on a golden throne, and that one can reach heaven only at the end of our life—but Amma says that this is not true. We can find heaven on earth, right here and now. It lies in the attitude of our own mind. We create our own heaven or hell. Amma wants us only to experience heaven.

Amma's wish for the world, and may it also be ours, is encapsulated in the mantra, *Om Lokah Samastah Sukhino Bhavantu*, (May the Whole World be Peaceful and Happy). Amma has repeated many times that She wants everyone to have a roof over their head. She believes that everyone should have at least one full meal each day. All should be able to go to sleep at night without fear. This is Amma's dream.

Our desires may consist of many different things, but Amma's desires are completely selfless and only for the betterment of the world. Amma has always lived Her life to the fullest extent in an effort to purify and uplift us, to inspire us to lead a good life. Amma is a living example of the qualities of humility and compassion, coupled with an overwhelming love for service to humanity.

It has been incredible to watch the flowers of Amma's mission bloom throughout the years. Everywhere we travel in India we can see the physical manifestation of Her love in the form of various educational institutions, hospitals, housing projects, and so many more endeavors that it is impossible to mention them all.

Amma's institutions have achieved the reputation of having first class technology and selfless workers, but Amma will never take the credit for building up Her ashram or for all of the activities that have begun in Her name. When questioned about these incredible achievements, Amma humbly answers, "I don't lay any claims to having done anything. It is my children who have made all this possible. My children are my wealth—they are my strength."

Amma further explains that She attributes all of the ashram's success to the renunciation and selfless effort of Her devotees. She has never spent time calculating whether a project is feasible or not before starting it. It is the need of the people that is the starting point for all Her humanitarian activities. When Amma has felt their need, She has committed, and with God's grace things have always come together whenever She has felt inspired to undertake a project.

Amma's organization is highly effective because it relies upon the voluntary efforts of Her devotees. When other organizations allocate money for relief projects, most of it is dissipated in wages and administrative costs. The situation is like pouring oil from one glass to another down a line—in the end,

there is hardly any oil left. Most of it has been lost, sticking to the sides of all the glasses. In this way 1000 rupees diminishes to ten rupees by the time it reaches the people. On the other hand if we are given ten rupees, we add our effort to it and the money multiplies. This is the power of selfless giving: one can start with two cents and end up with a dollar.

There is a circle of love in selfless giving. The circle is complete when those who have received Amma's love at a distance finally meet Her. Then She Herself lets them know directly that the love they are feeling is real, long-lasting, and a part of their own true nature. By bestowing love on us, Amma awakens love within us.

Amma's inspiration becomes like a divine accelerator. Once pressed, it runs almost of its own accord with tremendous power. It is a power that comes not from domination but from love. It is the opposite of our everyday concepts of power. This love is the key to our spiritual growth, and to the changes Amma can make in us. Only in selfless love do we find enough courage and patience to guide us through difficult times.

For every individual who is directly touched by Amma's love, there are many, many more who receive the benefit of that touch. Amma inspires very ordinary people to do extraordinary things. Their enthusiasm is not just to do social service, nor is it simply an idea to "do good." It is much more; it is the devotees' way of expressing their love for Amma.

We can have a relationship with Amma wherever we may be, for Amma tells us that She is always with us. A young girl had a strong desire to meet Amma, but was not able to go to Amritapuri to do so. She worked as a servant in a very strict household and could not ask for time away from her job. She tried to associate with people who had met Amma and who would speak of Her, and was happy when one day she received a small photograph of Amma. Still, her desire to meet Amma and have Her darshan remained strong. One evening several people from her town were going to the ashram for Amma's Devi Bhava program, and they invited her to join them. The girl was unable to get permission to go with them and was heartbroken.

When the owners of the house left that evening, the girl laid her head down on the floor and cried. Suddenly she felt someone's presence in the room. She raised her head and was overwhelmed to see Amma dressed as Devi sitting on the couch, wearing a green sari and the crown and jewelry of the Divine Mother. There was a very special fragrance around Her. The girl thought perhaps she was dreaming but knew she was wide-awake. Amma lifted her from the floor, wiped her tears, and put her head on Her shoulder, saying, "My darling daughter, don't cry. I'm always with you." She held her hand and looked deeply into her eyes, and then suddenly disappeared.

When her friends returned the following day, the girl asked them what color sari Amma had worn for Devi Bhava. They confirmed that Amma had indeed worn green. It has been four years since she had this miraculous vision of Amma, and even though she has never made it to Amritapuri to meet Amma in person, she knows in her heart that Amma is always with her.

In India, the teachings of God-realized Masters have formed the foundation of Sanatana Dharma. The vibrations of their realization and the great truths they have spoken are still present in a subtle form. Amma is the crown jewel of that ancient unbroken lineage.

When Amma was sixteen, Her younger brother saw Her sitting by the backwaters crying. At first he thought that She was crying because somebody had reprimanded or beaten Her, and he went to ask Her what had happened. Amma looked at him and said, "Son, I can feel the sorrows of the world. I can hear the cry of suffering humanity, and I also know the way to remove their sorrows." This compassion has manifested through Her life and is the foundation for all of Her actions as She tries to reach out to us again and again.

It may be difficult to imagine that Amma knows each and everyone's heart and our deepest desires when She has millions of children all over the world. But She shows each one of us time and time again, that She has the capacity to hear us, to know us on the deepest level.

Amma once said, "My children think I do not remember them, but every night Amma goes to each one of Her children all around the world and kisses them goodnight."

Some people talk about a golden age to come. I believe that with Amma's birth on this earth, it has come. The grace we have to have Amma with us—is incomprehensible. In life, we all search for a piece of heaven on earth. I know where I have found mine!

Inside this impure world lies the bliss
of You in all of creation.
My heart trembles with anticipation
at the thought of beholding
Your precious form.
This one desire keeps me holding on —
as the days drift emptily by.

When will dawn the day
when the clouds of delusion subside?
Your sweet promise makes me thirsty
to drink of Your form.
With the thought of You before me held firmly,
I realize I know nothing.
To seek anything else becomes vain.

One touch of Your lotus feet will free me,
And I shall gladly drown in Your sea of compassion.

Glossary

Adivasi: Original inhabitants of the land.

AIMS: Amrita Institute of Medical Sciences. Amma's multi-specialty hospital in Cochin.

Amritapuri: Amma's main ashram headquarters in Kerala, India.

Amritavarsham50: Four-day event for world peace and harmony held in Cochin in 2003, for Amma's 50th birthday celebration.

Arati: Waving the burning camphor with ringing of bells at the end of worship representing the complete offering of the ego to God.

Archana: Recitation of names of God.

Arjuna: A famous warrior prince. The beloved disciple to whom Sri Krishna imparted the teaching of the *Bhagavad Gita* around 3000 B.C.

Ashram: A residential community where spiritual discipline is practiced; the abode of a saint.

Atman: The Supreme Self or Consciousness. Denotes both the Supreme Soul and the individual soul.

Ayurveda: The ancient traditional Indian system of medicine.

Bhajans: Devotional singing.

Bhava: Divine mood or attitude.

Brahmachari: A celibate male disciple who practices spiritual disciplines.

Brahmacharini: The female equivalent of a brahmachari.

Buttermilk: Drink made from yogurt and water.

Chai: Indian tea boiled with milk.

Chatti: Round metal bowl used in construction work to carry things.

Darshan: Vision of the Divine or audience with a holy person.

Devi: Divine Mother.

Dharma: Duty or righteous responsibility.

Dhoti: Piece of cloth wrapped around the waist usually worn by men.

Dowry: Financial arrangement of money and gifts given from the bride's family to her husband and his family.

Ego: Limited "I"-awareness, which identifies with limiting attributes such as the body or the mind.

Gopis: Cowherd girls and milkmaids who lived in Vrindavan. They were Krishna's closest devotees known for their supreme devotion.

Gunas: Qualities (Sattva, Rajas, Tamas). The three qualities of matter or energy that make up the phenomenal world.

Guru: A spiritual teacher.

Gurudev: "Divine Teacher," a customary Sanskrit term of respect used to address the spiritual teacher.

IAM: Integrated Amrita Meditation technique developed by Amma.

Japa: Repetition of a mantra.

Kalari: The small temple where Amma originally held the Bhava Darshans.

Karma Yoga: The path of action through selfless service.

Karma: Action or deed. Also the chain of effects that our actions produce.

Krishna: The eighth incarnation of Lord Vishnu whose teachings are contained in the *Bhagavad Gita*.

Kurukshetra: The field where the Mahabharata battle took place. At this place Sri Krishna imparted the teaching of the *Bhagavad Gita* to Arjuna.

Mahatma: Literally "Great Soul." A Hindu title of respect for a spiritually elevated person. In this book, Mahatma refers to a God-realized soul.

Mala: Garland or necklace.

Malayalam: Amma's mother tongue. The language of Kerala.

Mantra: A sacred sound or group of words with the power to transform.

Maya: Illusion.

Om Amriteshwaryai Namaha: Mantra meaning "Salutations to the Goddess of Immortality."

Om Namah Shivaya: Powerful mantra with different interpretations, usually meaning, "I bow down to the Eternally Auspicious One."

Pada puja: Traditional worship ceremony of washing the Guru's feet.

Panchakarma: The five different cleansing techniques used in Ayurvedic treatment.

Pappadam: Very popular, thin, round, crisp food item usually served with rice.

Paramatman: The Supreme Soul or God.

Prasad: A blessed offering or gift from a holy person or temple.

Puja: Ceremonial worship.

Pujari: Temple priest who performs traditional worship.

Punyam: Merit.

Radha: One of the gopis. She was the closest one to Krishna and personifies the highest and purest love for God.

Rajas: Activity, passion; one of the three basic qualities of nature that determine the inherent characteristics of all created things.

Rudraksha: Seed of a tree usually grown in Nepal that is known for its medicinal and spiritual power. Legendarily known as "teardrops of Lord Shiva."

Sadhana: Spiritual practices that lead to the goal of Self-realization.

Samadhi: Oneness with God. A transcendental state in which one loses all sense of individual identity.

Sanatana Dharma: Literally "eternal religion." The original and traditional name for Hinduism.

Sankalpa: A resolve.

Sannyas: Ceremony where formal vows of renunciation are taken.

Sanskrit: Ancient Indian language, said to be the language of the Gods.

Satsang: Listening to a spiritual talk or discussion; the company of saints and devotees.

Seva: Selfless service.

Shraddha: Care, attentiveness, faith.

Swami: One who takes the monastic vows of celibacy and renunciation.

Swamini: A female monastic.

Tapas: Austerity, hardship undergone for the sake of self-purification.

Tulasi: Holy basil, a medicinal plant.

Tyagam: To give up; renunciation.

Vairagya: Detachment, dispassion.

Vasanas: Residual impressions of objects and actions experienced, latent tendencies.

Vedanta: A system of philosophy mainly based upon the teachings of the *Upanishads*, the *Bhagavad Gita*, and the *Brahma Sutras*, discussing the nature of the Self.

Vibhuti: Sacred ash, usually given by Amma as prasad.

Vrindavan: The place where Sri Krishna lived as a young boy.